# *Using the* INTERNET

101 ESSENTIAL TIPS

# Using the INTERNET

TECHNICAL CONSULTANT
Chris Lewis

FENN

A DK PUBLISHING BOOK

**Editor** Irene Lyford
**Art Editor** Alan McKee
**Series Editor** Gillian Roberts
**Series Art Editor** Clive Hayball
**Production Controller** Lauren Britton
**US Editor** Laaren Brown

The full names of certain products referred to in this book are: Microsoft® MS-DOS®, Microsoft® Windows® 95, MSN™, The Microsoft®Network, Microsoft® Internet Gaming Zone, Microsoft® Internet Explorer. Netscape Communications, the Netscape Communications logo, Netscape & Netscape Navigator are trademarks of Netscape Communications Corporation.
*Every effort has been made to trace the copyright holders. The publisher apologizes for any unintentional omissions and would be pleased, in such cases, to place an acknowledgment in future editions of this book.*

First published in Canada in 1997 by
Fenn Publishing Company Limited,
34 Nixon Road, Toronto, Ontario L7E 1W2, Canada



Visit Dorling Kindersley on the World Wide Web at http://www.dk.com


Published in Great Britain by Dorling Kindersley Limited.

ISBN 1-55168-101-3

Text film output by The Right Type, Great Britain
Reproduced by Colourscan
Printed and bound in Italy by Graphicom

# 101 ESSENTIAL TIPS

PAGES 8-11

## UNDERSTANDING THE INTERNET



PAGES 12-22

## GETTING CONNECTED

PAGES 23-29

## SENDING & RECEIVING E-MAIL



PAGES 30-37

## DOWNLOADING FILES

PAGES 38-49

## THE WORLD WIDE WEB

PAGES 50-52

## LOGGING ON WITH TELNET



PAGES 53-57

## NEWSGROUPS ON THE INTERNET



PAGES 58-69

## ON-LINE CHATTING

# UNDERSTANDING THE INTERNET

## 1 WHAT IS THE INTERNET?

The Internet is a worldwide network of computers holding vast quantities of data accessible directly from a home computer. Access to the Internet is channeled through the high-speed links provided by commercial organizations known as service providers. Although the volume and variety of information may seem overwhelming, the basic processes are quite simple: you do not need to be a computer expert to enjoy the Internet.

***Files & software*** *that are publicly available on the Internet can be accessed and downloaded using FTP (File Transfer Protocol).*

***Electronic mail (e-mail)*** *is a fast and economical way to send messages to anyone with an Internet account. Messages can include text, pictures, and even audio or animation.*

YOUR PLACE IN THE NET
*Once you have connected your computer to a modem and signed up with a service provider, you can select which software to use and start exploring the Net. As you become more experienced, you will discover the areas that appeal to you.*

***An individual*** *can access data and communicate with others worldwide from his or her computer.*

***Over 15,000 discussion groups*** *exist on the Net. In these, you can participate in discussions on different topics and also receive information about specialized subjects by subscribing to mailing lists.*

***Numerous colorful sites*** *make up the World Wide Web; Web browser software lets you navigate around them. Many Web pages are interactive, allowing you to move from one site to another by clicking on a "hot" word or icon.*

***On-line chatting,*** *where individuals are able to to communicate "live" with each other via their computer keyboards, is a hugely popular activity on the Internet.*

***Users*** *receive their link to the Internet, e-mail addresses, and telephone access numbers from one or more of the thousands of commercial service providers.*

## ? IS IT WORLDWIDE?

Technically, anyone with a computer and modem can telephone a service provider and access the Net, but some countries have few service providers and limited local coverage. Access will also depend, to a degree, on the sophistication of a country's telephone system.

# 3 WHAT CAN YOU DO ON THE INTERNET?

Once you are connected to the Internet, you join a global community of over 50 million users with whom you can communicate "live" or by sending e-mail messages; you can subscribe to newsgroups or mailing lists and engage in on-line shopping; and you can access any of the huge amount of electronic data stored on the computers that make up the Internet.

△ VISITING INTERNET SITES
*To visit Internet sites with a Web browser such as* Netscape Navigator, *just type the address and press the Return or Enter key.*

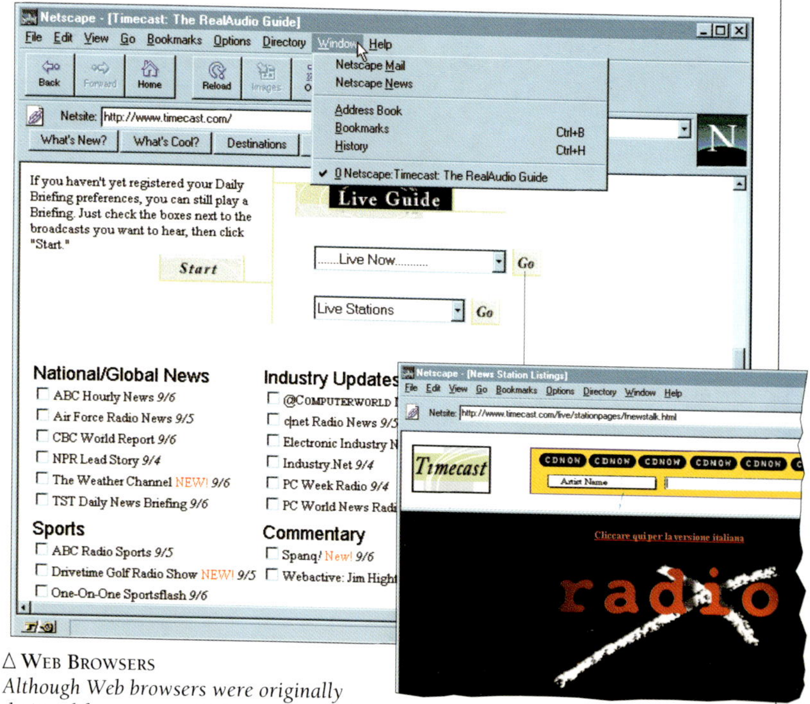


△ WEB BROWSERS
*Although Web browsers were originally designed for accessing Web pages, today's powerful versions are more versatile and provide newcomers with an excellent method of exploring the Internet.*

△ SURFING BETWEEN SITES
*On the* Timecast *page, click the* Go *button to access a menu of live audio sites. Click on a menu option to access a site.*

## 4 UNDERSTANDING NETWORKS

At the Internet's core is a network of supercomputers (represented on the illustration by red dots) that are connected to each other by high-speed links (the white lines) known as "backbones." Each node is linked to a number of smaller networks. These are linked to even smaller networks and, ultimately, to your computer.

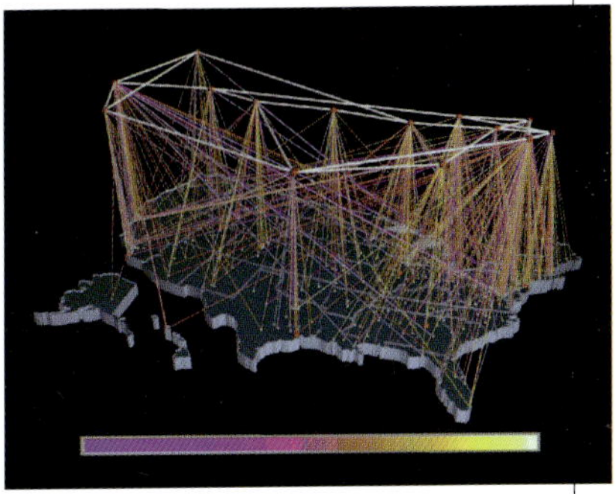

THE MAIN US NETWORK – NSFNET

## 5 ESSENTIAL JARGON

Newcomers to the Internet are often bewildered by the acronyms, abbreviations, and the seemingly incomprehensible terminology that abounds. Below is a glossary of some of the most common terms.

- **Anonymous FTP**
A way of logging on to a remote computer using an FTP program.
- **Archie**
A database of files stored on FTP sites.
- **BBS**
A single computer or network that you dial direct to access services (*Tip 18*).
- **Client/Server**
Computers within a network are either clients, which request information, or servers, which store and deliver information.
- **FTP**
A protocol for transferring files on the Internet (*Tip 37*).
- **IRC**
Networks on the Net where you hold "live" conversations with other users (*Tip 80*).
- **ISDN**
A communication standard allowing a telephone line to carry digital data at speeds higher than is possible with a modem (*Tip 6*).
- **Newbie**
A user who is new to the Internet.
- **PoP**
The telephone number that customers use to dial in to their service provider (*Tip 21*).
- **URL (Uniform Resource Locator)**
An Internet address, providing a standard way of referring to Internet resources.
- **Usenet**
The main network of newsgroups available on the Internet.
- **Web browser**
A program for viewing and accessing data on the World Wide Web.

# GETTING CONNECTED

## 6 WHAT IS NEEDED TO GET CONNECTED?

To connect to the Internet you need a computer (any fairly new computer should be suitable, as long as it has enough power and memory); a modem to convert data into a form that can be transmitted over the telephone network; and an account with a service provider who will supply the link between your computer and the Internet.

**WHAT IS ISDN?**
*The Integrated Services Digital Network lets you send digital information at very high speeds over existing telephone lines, providing the fastest link to the Internet. However, you need a special telephone connection and can use it only if your service provider also has an ISDN link.*

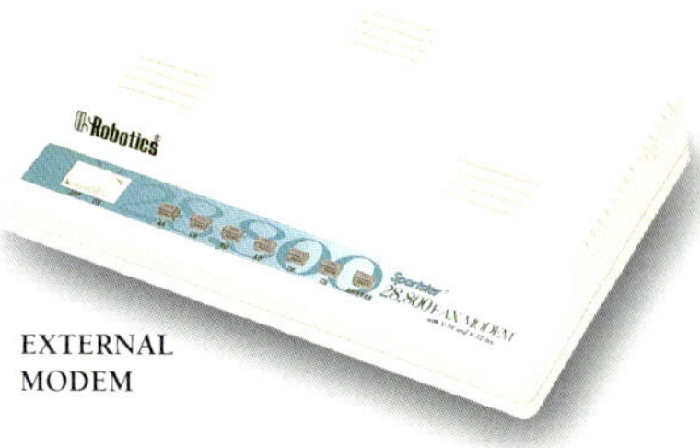


EXTERNAL MODEM

**ALL-IN-ONE INTERNET KITS ▽**
*Starter kits are popular with beginners and usually contain a modem, cable and adapter, software, and a manual. Some kits also include a free trial account with a reputable service provider.*

## 7 MINIMUM REQUIREMENTS

Although many people access the Internet with slower computers, you will need an IBM-compatible PC with at least a 486 processor, or a Macintosh Performa series or higher, and 8 (preferably 16) MB RAM to explore effectively the features described in this book.

## 8 CHECK THE SPEED OF YOUR SERIAL PORT

To use an external 28.8K modem effectively, you need a 16550 UART chip in your serial port. If you have bought a 28.8K modem and your computer uses a slower chip, it will perform only as well as a 14.4K modem. Resolve this difficulty by installing a fast serial card in one of the expansion slots inside your computer.

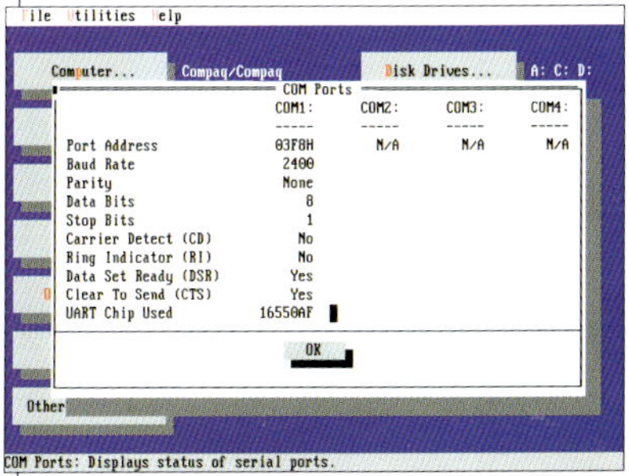


◁ CHECK THE UART CHIP SPEED

- *Restart your computer in MS-DOS mode by checking box in* Shut Down Window *dialog box.*
- *When DOS prompt (C:>) appears, type* **msd** *and press Return. Now click* COM Ports *button.*
- *Read information on* UART Chip Used *line. If this shows the number 16550, you have a fast enough serial port to run a 28.8K modem. If you see only 8250, you will need to consider an upgrade.*

## 9 HOW A MODEM WORKS

A modem (the term is simply a contraction of Modulator-Demodulator) is a device that converts data from the binary code used by your computer to an analog signal that can be transmitted over the telephone network, and vice versa.

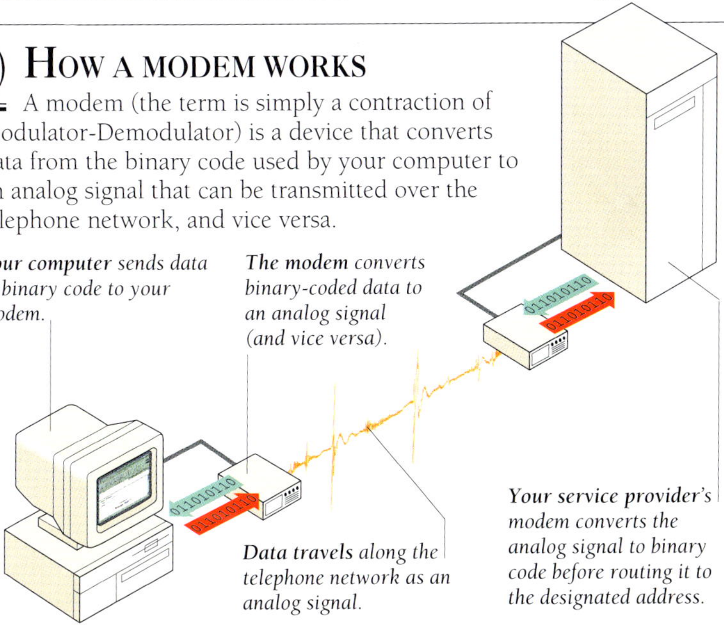


***Your computer** sends data in binary code to your modem.*

***The modem** converts binary-coded data to an analog signal (and vice versa).*

***Data travels** along the telephone network as an analog signal.*

***Your service provider's** modem converts the analog signal to binary code before routing it to the designated address.*

## 10 CHOOSING A MODEM

Modems exist in a variety of shapes and sizes, but the basic choice is between external, internal, and card versions. After deciding which of those is most suited to your needs, consider price, speed, and compatibility. Computer and Internet magazines are good sources of reviews and information about what is available.

**FAX MODEMS**
*Most modems come with software enabling them to be used to receive and send faxes, but* Windows 95 *also includes a fax program* (Microsoft Fax) *with its modem utilities.*

△ EXTERNAL MODEM
*Simple to connect, external modems are available in many different designs.*

△ CARD MODEM
*Ideal for installation in a notebook PC, this modem is the size of a credit card.*

△ INTERNAL MODEM
*An internal modem fits into an expansion slot inside your computer.*

## 11 WHEN IS MODEM SPEED IMPORTANT?

Although the importance of speed depends on how you plan to use your modem, it is generally advisable to buy the fastest model you can afford. This is especially true if you intend to explore the World Wide Web and to download a lot of files. Modem speed is also an important factor in reducing your on-line telephone charges.

## 12 INTERNAL OR EXTERNAL MODEM?

There are several factors you need to consider when choosing a modem. Bear in mind that it can be a complicated business to install an internal modem, so if you are new to computers or inexperienced, an external modem (which is simple to connect) may be the best choice.

- An internal modem takes up no desk space and needs no cable or electrical outlet.
- An external modem needs cable and an electrical outlet. Indicator lights on its case show the status of your Internet session and it is easy to move to another computer.

◁ INTERNAL MODEM

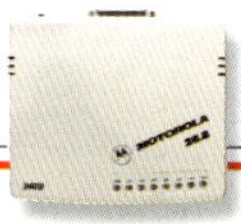

◁ EXTERNAL MODEM

## 13 CONNECTING AN INTERNAL MODEM

If you are a beginner or in any way uncertain, do not try to install an internal modem yourself, but ask your dealer to do it for you. An internal modem is a card that is fitted into a vacant expansion slot on your computer's motherboard. After installation of an internal modem card, it may be necessary to adjust the *Windows 95* settings.

## 14 CONNECTING AN EXTERNAL MODEM

Connecting an external modem is usually a straightforward task. First, connect your modem to the power supply, using the cable provided; this may include a power adapter. Now attach one end of the serial cable to the modem, and the other end to a vacant serial port on your computer; this will usually be the COM 1 port, but if a mouse is already connected there, use COM 2. Plug the telephone cable into a phone jack and then switch on the modem. Some of the indicator lights should light up.

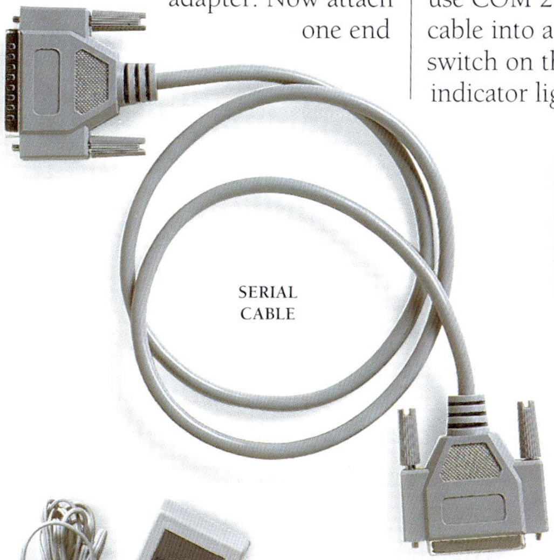


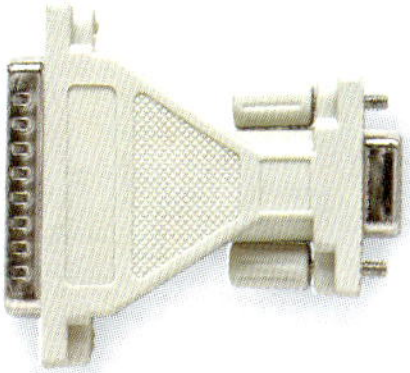

△ SERIAL CABLE ADAPTER
*An adapter cable or plug converts a 25-pin plug to fit a 9-pin socket.*

**AVOID SCREECHING**
*External modems can emit an unpleasant screeching sound when establishing connections. Avoid this by choosing a modem with a built-in volume control.*

◁ AC POWER ADAPTER
*Your modem may have a built-in power cable, with adapter; otherwise, plug the cable in with a jack.*

# 15 HOW TO CONFIGURE A MODEM IN WINDOWS® 95

Having connected your external modem, you can now configure it in *Windows 95*. First, make sure that the modem is connected to a power supply and switched on (at least one of the indicator lights should be lit), then follow the steps below. Although it is possible for *Windows 95* to detect automatically the make and model of your modem, it is simple to do it manually.

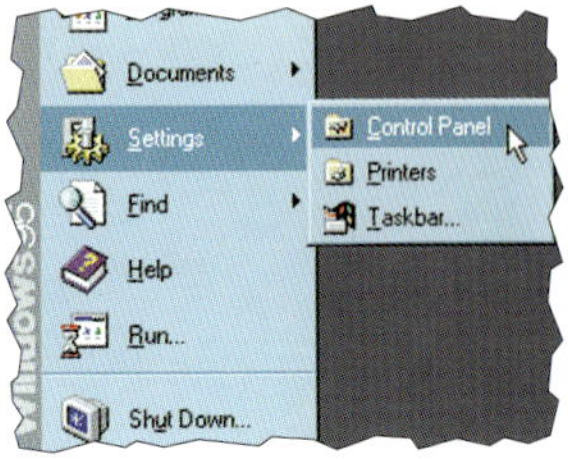


1 △ From *Start* button, go to *Settings* and then to *Control Panel*.

2 △ Double-click on *Modems* icon; *Install New Modem* window will now appear.

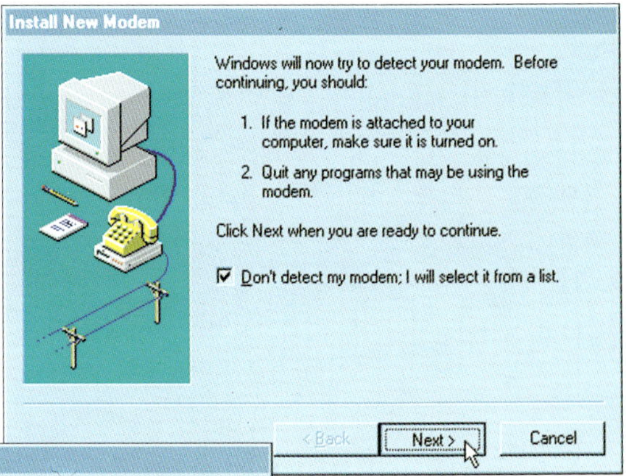


3 △ Read and follow instructions in box, then check box next to *Don't detect my modem; I will select it from a list.* Now click *Next*.

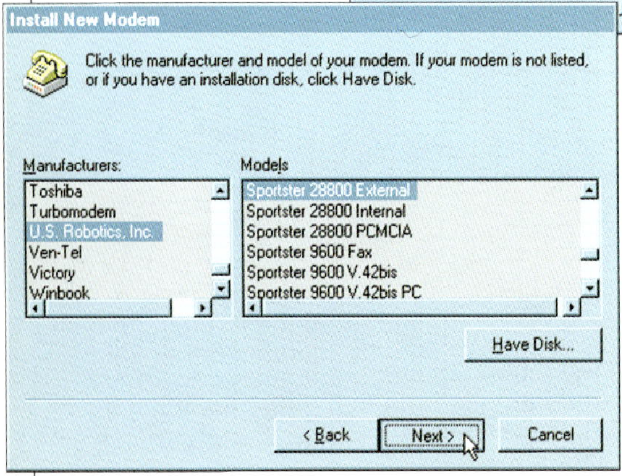


4 ◁ Using vertical scroll bars, select appropriate make and model of your modem in *Manufacturers* box and then in *Models* box. Click *Next*.

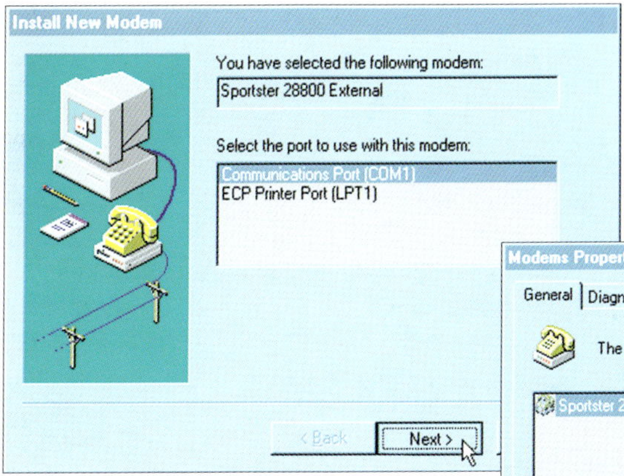


5 ◁ Now choose appropriate port in *Select the port to use with this modem* panel, then click *Next*. When message box appears, click *Finish*.

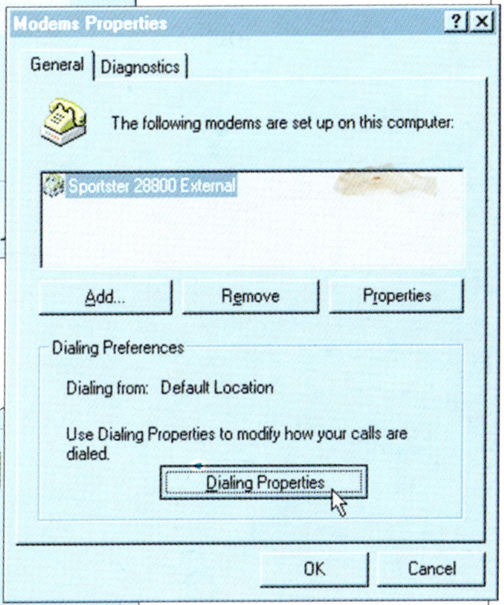


6 ▷ In *Modems Properties* box, which will now appear on *General* page, click *Dialing Properties* button.

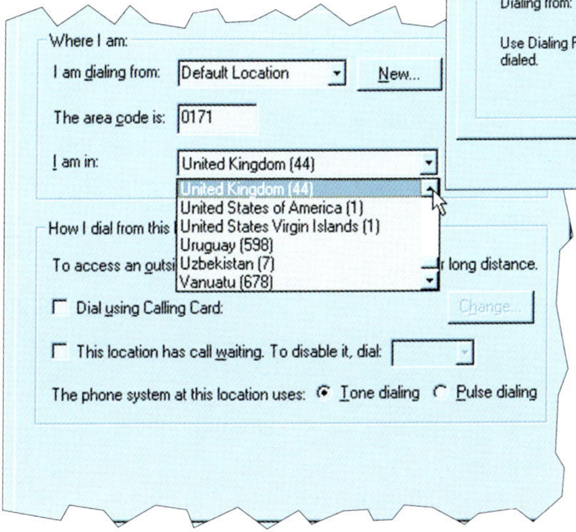


7 △ Type appropriate information in box next to *The area code is*. Click arrow on right of box next to *I am in*, and choose your country from drop-down list. Click *OK* and, finally, click *OK* in *Modems Properties* dialog box. Your modem is now ready to use.

STILL HAVING PROBLEMS?

*If your modem does not appear in the lists at Step 4, let* Windows 95 *try to detect it automatically: it will probably select* Standard Modem Types, *which should get you up and running. If you were supplied with a disk with a* Windows 95 *driver, at Step 4, click* Have disk *button and navigate to floppy disk drive. Click on the appropriate file.*

## 16 TELEPHONE TIPS

If you use the "call waiting" facility with your telephone, you must disable it before starting a modem session, since the beep that announces an incoming call could disrupt data transfer. To do this, check the box next to *This location has call waiting* in the *Dialing Properties* dialog box (Steps 6 & 7, *Tip 15*). You'll have to contact your telephone company to find out what to put in the box next to *To disable it, dial ...*

DISABLE CALL WAITING

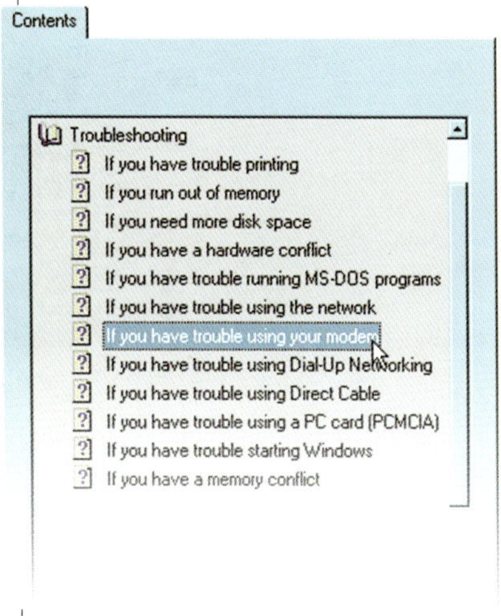


MODEM TROUBLESHOOTING

## 17 MODEM HELP & ADVICE

The *Windows 95* help system offers useful on-line advice on modem problems. For difficulties with installation, access *Windows Help* and click on *I don't know how to install my modem*: this will take you through the process step by step.

- For other problems, choose *Help* from the *Start* menu, double-click *Troubleshooting* in the *Contents* page, then double-click on *If you have trouble using your modem.*
- Your modem supplier should be able to advise you about *Windows 95*-compatible modem drivers.

## 18 DIAL A BBS TO TEST YOUR MODEM

Once you have installed and configured your modem, you can test it by dialing a Bulletin Board Service. All you need is a telephone number for a BBS (these are often advertised in computer magazines) and the *Windows 95* accessory called *HyperTerminal*. Many BBSs are commercial, but others are free services run by enthusiasts.

## 19 CONNECT TO A BBS WITH HYPERTERMINAL

The first time you make a BBS connection, *HyperTerminal* will prompt you for information about dialing properties and modem settings, enabling you to assign an icon and a name to each connection. Future connections can then be made by double-clicking the relevant icon in the *HyperTerminal* window. Install *HyperTerminal* from your *Windows 95* installation CD or disks, using the *Add/Remove Programs* utility.

1 ◁ From *Start* menu choose *Programs*, then select *Accessories*. Double-click *Hypertrm* icon in *HyperTerminal* window.

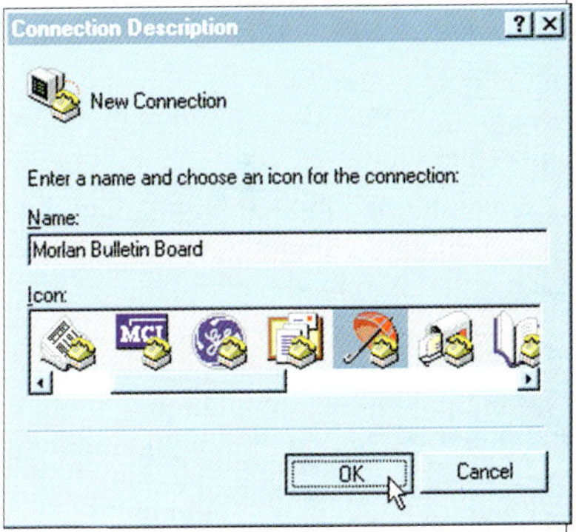


2 △ In *Connection Description* dialog box, type name of BBS you want to call in *Name* box. Click an icon in *Icon* box. Click *OK*. Icon and name will now appear in *HyperTerminal* window.

3 ◁ In *Phone Number* dialog box, choose relevant country code, then type area code and telephone number for Bulletin Board Service you want to call. Click *OK*. A *Connect* box will appear. Click *Dial* to connect to BBS.

## 20 ACCESSING THE INTERNET

To gain access to the Internet, you must first open an account with a service (or access) provider. There are many such companies, each offering slightly different services, at different costs. There are two main categories: Internet Service Providers and On-line Service Providers (*Tips 21 & 22*). Both offer Internet access, but the latter also provides exclusive information and services.

# 21 INTERNET SERVICE PROVIDERS

There are dozens of Internet service providers, offering a range of services. Some just provide a connection to the Internet and software to dial the nearest PoP, leaving you to download the software you need from an FTP site (*Tip 37*). Others offer a more comprehensive package, including a Web browser, e-mail program, and FTP program. Costs vary, but most providers charge a sign-up fee, then a fixed monthly or annual fee for unlimited access to the Internet.

**WHAT IS A POP?**
*PoPs are local telephone access numbers offered by service providers. The extent of PoP coverage offered varies greatly, and this is a factor to consider when deciding which provider to sign up with. If you can dial a PoP at local call rates, you will be able to use the Internet at that rate.*

**INTERNET ACCESS**
*If your ISP offers direct Internet connection, you can run any Internet software, such as the latest Web browsers.*

**ON-LINE CHARGES**
*Most Internet service providers charge a flat monthly or annual fee that gives you unlimited access to the Internet, with no extra charges.*

**POP COVERAGE**
*The major ISPs usually provide excellent PoP coverage in their own countries, but access from abroad may be difficult.*

**NO EXTRA CONTENT**
*Internet service providers offer no extra content: they simply provide access to the Internet as a whole, which you then use as you wish.*

### LOOK FOR SUPPORT

*Before signing up with a service provider, check how much support they offer to users. On-line service providers, such as* CompuServe, *provide free telephone support, which can be invaluable for newcomers. Few ISPs offered such support in the past, but the situation is now improving.*

## 22 ON-LINE SERVICE PROVIDERS

The main commercial on-line service providers, such as *CompuServe* and *America Online* (*AOL*), offer vast databases of information, including news, weather, and software support, as well as simple access to the Internet via a number of easy-to-follow screens. The trend among on-line service providers such as *America Online*, which has the greatest number of subscribers, is to adopt a flat-rate pricing model, charging a fixed monthly rate for unlimited hours on line.

### INTERNET ACCESS

*Easy access to the Internet is built into the software provided, so you can, for example, launch a Web browser or access an FTP site simply by clicking a button.*

### USEFUL DATABASES

*On-line service providers give you reliable, wide-ranging on-line databases, as well as access to other services and sources of information.*

### ON-LINE CHARGES

*Although precise charges and billing procedures vary, the trend is for on-line service providers to charge a fixed monthly rate for unlimited usage.*

### POP COVERAGE

*The major on-line service providers are US-based and offer worldwide PoP coverage, so it is simple to access your account when not at home.*

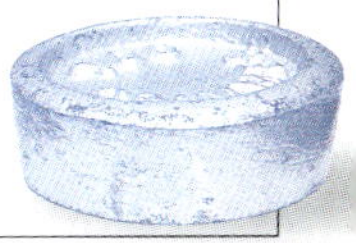

## 23 TRY BEFORE YOU BUY

Free trial accounts are frequently offered – as part of a modem package, for example, or on CD-ROMs given away by computer magazines. These offer a way of trying out different service providers before signing up. Be sure to check the small print carefully, however, to avoid being billed for use after the trial period.

△ FREE TRIAL ACCOUNT OFFERS

CYBERIA CAFÉ, PARIS

◁ INTERNET CAFÉS
*Sometimes known as cybercafés, these provide an excellent opportunity to find out what the Internet has to offer and to experiment with the services available. Experts are on hand to assist you, and training courses are usually available.*

## 24 ASK BEFORE SIGNING UP

Get as much information as possible before signing up with a service provider. Below are some of the important questions to ask.

**How much will it cost?**
- What is the registration fee?
- Does the monthly fee give unlimited Internet access?

**What is the extent of PoP coverage?**
- Is there a local PoP?
- Is national PoP coverage extensive?

**What support do you offer?**
- When are your telephone support lines open?

**Do you offer PPP (Point to Point Protocol) for Internet connection?**

CHECK COSTS

**What software is provided?**
- Web browser, FTP program, e-mail program, newsreader?
- Will the software be registered to me?
- Will the software install itself automatically?

**What sort of e-mail account will I have?**
- Do you offer POP3 (allowing access from any computer) or SMTP (Simple Mail Transfer Protocol) facilities?
- What would my e-mail address be?

# SENDING & RECEIVING E-MAIL

## 25 WHAT IS ELECTRONIC MAIL?

Using electronic mail (e-mail), you can send messages to anyone with an Internet account, and most businesses today have an electronic mailing address. Your e-mail message can include not just text but other files, such as images and spreadsheets. An even greater advantage is that your message can reach the recipient within minutes of being sent. Incoming messages are stored in your mailbox on your service provider's mail server until you next connect to the Internet.

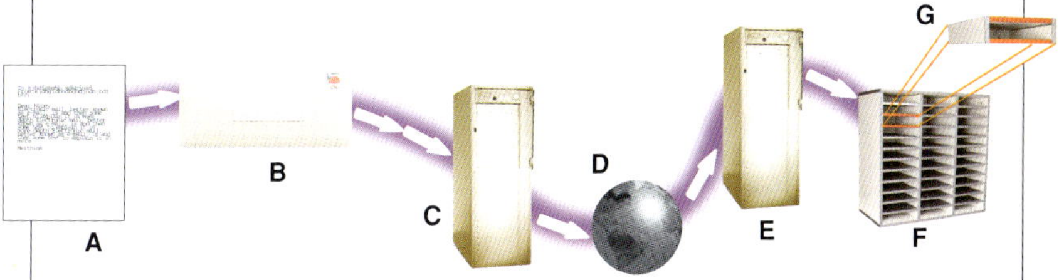


*There are many ways of sending and receiving electronic mail, but the basic process is the same.* **A** *Using a suitable e-mail program, you type your message.* **B** *Once you have addressed and sent your e-mail, it is encoded by a modem and sent down the telephone line as an analog signal.* **C** *The e-mail message arrives at your provider's server; if it recognizes the e-mail address as valid, the e-mail is sent.* **D** *The data is sent via the Internet.* **E** *The data is received by the recipient's provider and sent to his or her unique "pigeon hole."* **F** *Once your message reaches the host, it will remain there until the recipient next connects to the Internet.* **G** *Finally, the recipient's modem and computer decode the data and your e-mail message can be read as a text file.*

E-MAIL ADDRESSES

*The following Web sites list many addresses:*

**http://www.whowhere.com**
**http://okra.ucr.edu/okra**
**http://www.four11.com**

## 26 HOW TO DECIPHER AN E-MAIL ADDRESS

An e-mail address has two parts: the user name and a domain name, separated by an @ symbol. The number of domains in a name depends on how many branches are needed to sort it logically. Each address is unique and must be used exactly as given; adding spaces or changing from lower to upper case, or vice versa, may render it useless.

***Your user name** can be any name you choose, as long as it has not already been registered by another subscriber. You could use your full name, your first name, or an alias. Some service providers allocate numbers instead of names.*

***Your host name** is the name of your Internet service provider, the organization that provides you with Internet access and is responsible for sending and receiving messages to and from individual users.*

***The last section** of the domain name identifies your service provider's type of organization, and this may vary from one country to another. For example, in the US,* .com *indicates a commercial company, whereas the UK equivalent is* .co.

***The @ symbol** separates your user name from the domain name part of the address, which relates to your service provider.*

***The • symbol** separates the various domains of your address. Note that there is no space between the dot and adjacent letters.*

***A two-letter country code** forms the last part of the domain name of service providers based outside the US. For example, jp for Japan and fr for France.*

## 27 PROTECTING CONFIDENTIALITY

Be cautious about sending sensitive or confidential information via e-mail, since the contents could be read by anyone with access to the recipient's computer. If this is of concern, seek professional advice about the possibility of protecting your mail with special software.

## 28 DEDICATED E-MAIL PROGRAMS

There are many different ways of sending and receiving e-mail, including several dedicated e-mail programs. Qualcom's *Eudora*, one of the most widely used programs, is available in a freeware version (*Eudora Light*) from Qualcom's FTP site at **ftp.qualcomm.com**.

# 29 SETTING UP EUDORA

To use *Eudora* you need a POP3 account, which is a specific type of e-mail transfer protocol used by most service providers. If you are unsure about the type of e-mail account you have, check with your provider. When you first run *Eudora*, you will be asked to provide some configuration details, including your e-mail address and the name of your service provider's mail server. When you are ready, open the folder in which you have installed *Eudora* and follow these steps.

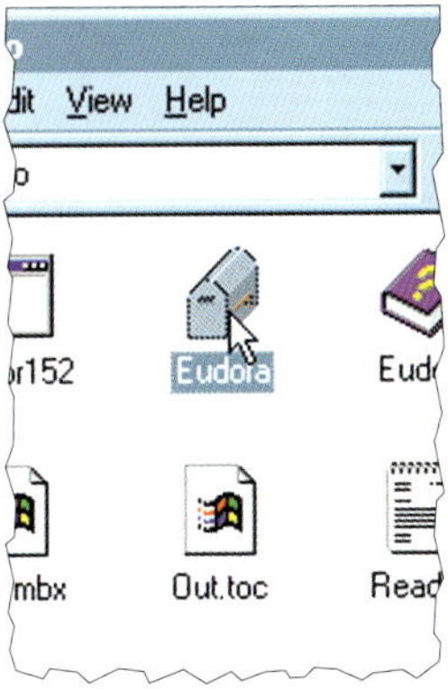


1 △ Double-click on *Eudora* icon: *Settings* dialog box will pop up with *Getting Started* highlighted.

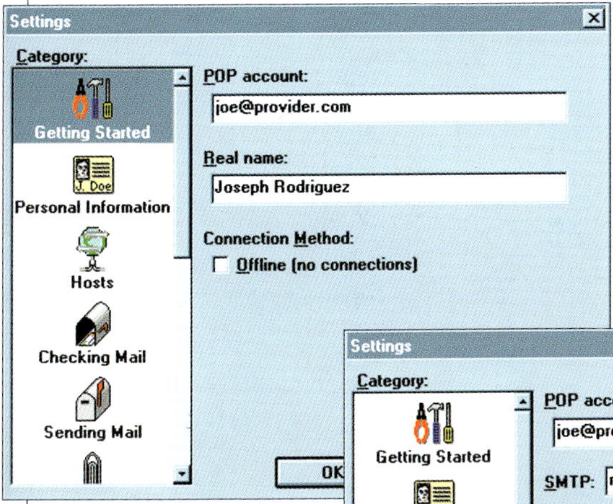


2 ◁ Type your e-mail address in *POP account* box. Type your name in *Real name* box.

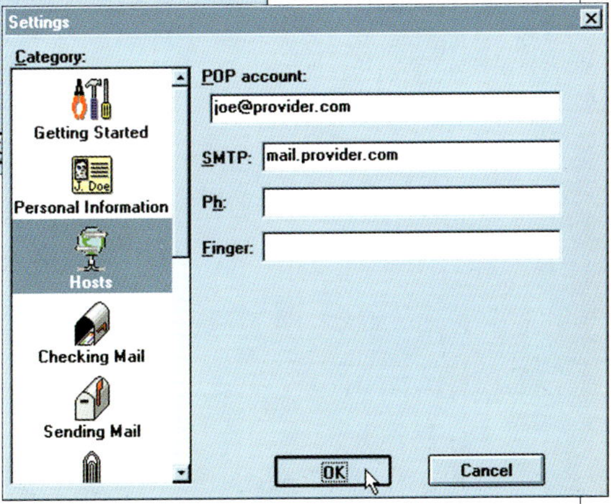


3 ▷ Click on *Hosts* in *Category* panel. *POP account* box will contain entry you made at Step 2. Type name of your service provider's mail server in *SMTP* box. Finally click *OK* to complete basic *Eudora* configuration.

# 30 SEND AN E-MAIL WITH EUDORA

Once you have configured the basic program settings, all you need to know is the e-mail address of the person to whom you want to send a message. After making your Internet connection, launch *Eudora*, then follow the steps below, which explain how to write and send a message while you are on-line. (It is also possible to write an e-mail off-line and send it later.)

1 △ Click *New Message* button. *No Recipient, No Subject* window will appear. Your details will already be displayed.

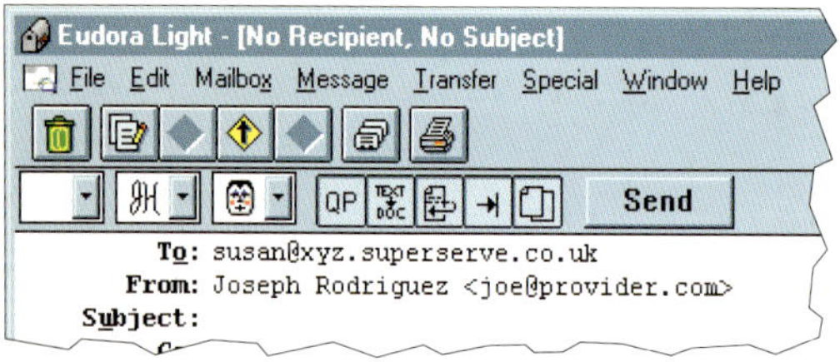


2 ◁ In *No Recipient, No Subject* window, place cursor alongside "To." Type e-mail address of recipient (normally in lower case letters). Press Tab key to move cursor alongside "Subject."

3 ▷ In Subject line, type brief description of subject of e-mail. Press Tab key three times. Now type your message.

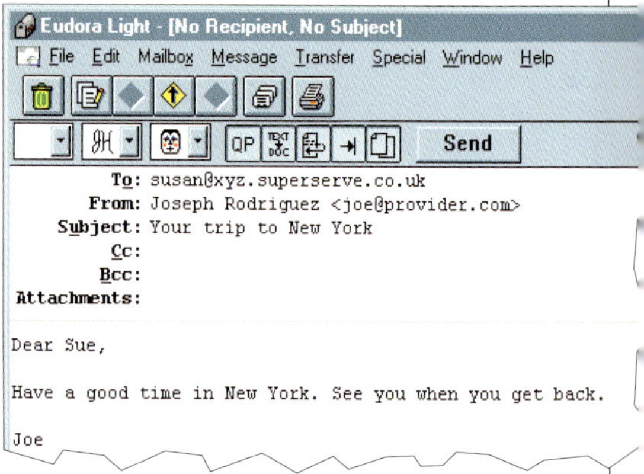

4 △ When ready to send your message, click *Send* button.

**WRITING MAIL OFF-LINE**

*If you process a lot of mail, write your messages off-line and place them in a queue (by pressing* Send *while off-line). When you are next on-line, send all the messages by choosing* Send Queued Messages *from the* File *menu.*

## 31 ATTACHING A DOCUMENT

Many e-mail programs allow you to send files from your hard disk by "attaching" them to your message. If you want to utilize this facility to attach a document to your message when you are using *Eudora*, before you click the *Send* button, choose *Attach File* from the *Message* menu. This opens the *Attach File* dialog box and lets you locate, on your hard disk, the document you want to attach to your message.

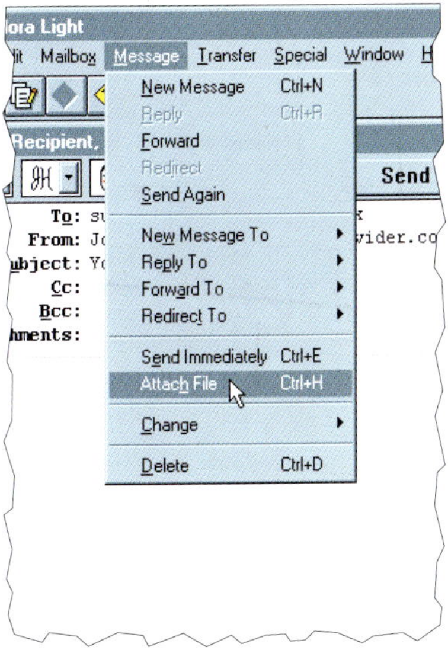

ATTACH A FILE

If a recipient is unable to view an attachment you have sent, ask which encoding method his or her e-mail program supports, because incompatibilities can occur. Three of the most common methods are MIME, UUEncode, and BINHEX.

**SENDING FILES BY E-MAIL**
*If you send a lot of large files, save time by using a compression program.*

## 32 CAN E-MAIL MESSAGES BE DELIVERED IF THE ADDRESS IS WRONG?

E-mail messages, like conventional mail, must be correctly addressed. If the computer trying to deliver your message does not recognize the mailing address, it will automatically send you a warning e-mail. You may see this message the next time you look in your mailbox, or perhaps several days later. In some systems, especially the on-line services, you can generate a receipt when your e-mail has been correctly delivered and read by the recipient.

**HELPFUL DESCRIPTIONS**
*Try to get into the habit of supplying a helpful subject description each time you send an e-mail message, particularly if you are posting to a mailing list. This will help recipients to decide whether a message needs immediate attention.*

# 33 RECEIVING E-MAIL WITH EUDORA

*Eudora* can be configured to alert you each time a new piece of mail arrives (as long as you are logged on to the Internet at the time). Choose *Settings* from the *Special* menu, then select *Getting Attention* from the *Category* panel. Highlight one of the three options and click *OK*. If you do not want to be alerted each time you receive a new message, you can choose to open a mailbox manually, following the steps below.

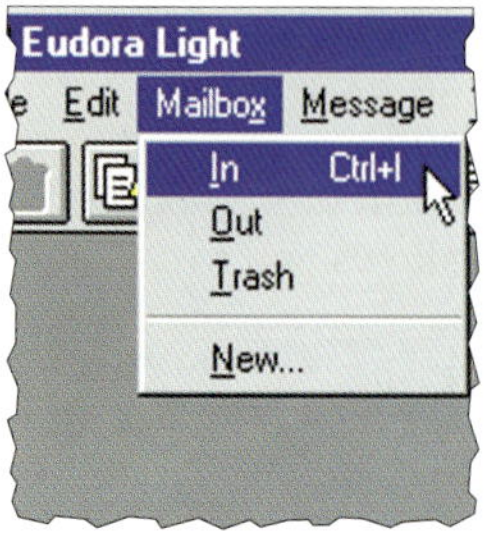


1 △ To read incoming e-mail, choose *In* from *Mailbox* menu. *In* window will appear.

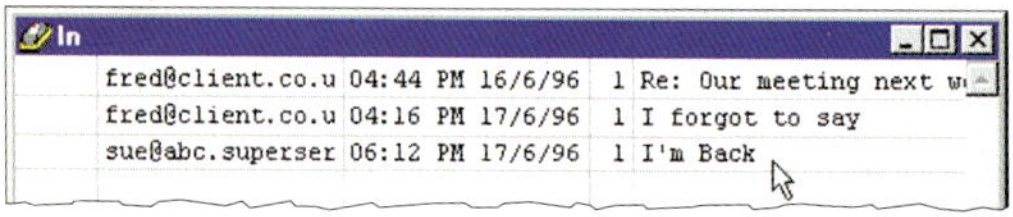


2 △ *In* window will contain details of all e-mail messages sent to your address. Double-click on any line to read selected message.

3 ▷ Chosen message will now appear in window. Title bar of window will contain your e-mail address and subject line of message.

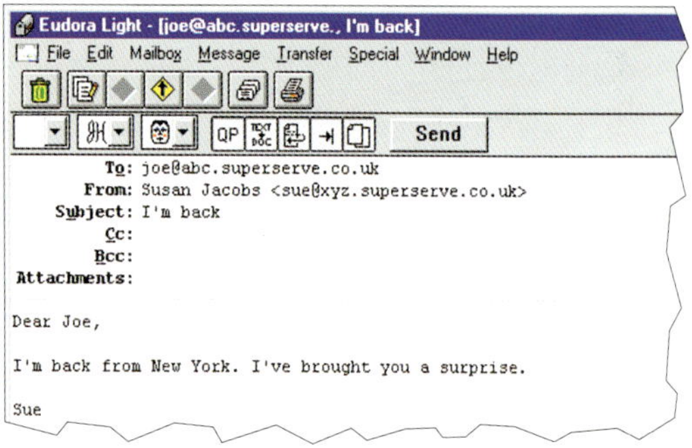


# 34 HOW TO REPLY TO AN E-MAIL MESSAGE

Choose *Eudora's Reply* command from the *Message* menu. This will produce a new message with the original text highlighted and indented, with angled brackets. Keep the original text in your reply: the angled brackets will distinguish your response from the original message.

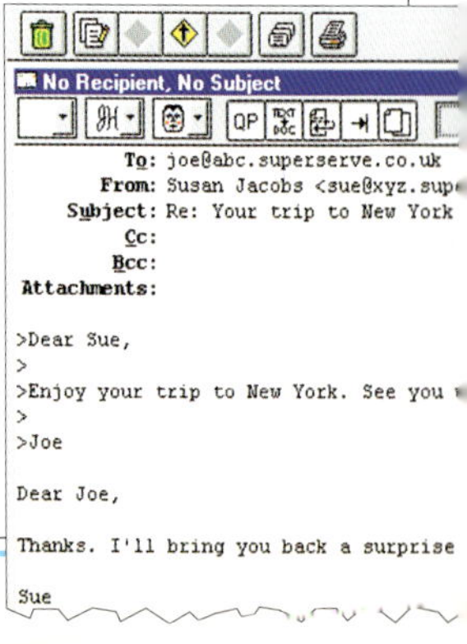


E-MAIL MESSAGE & REPLY

# 35 STORING E-MAIL ADDRESSES

Most e-mail programs have an address book facility for storing and managing your list of e-mail addresses. *Eudora*'s address book allows you to select addresses from a drop-down menu when you want to send a new message. The steps below explain how to add the e-mail address on an outgoing message to your address book.

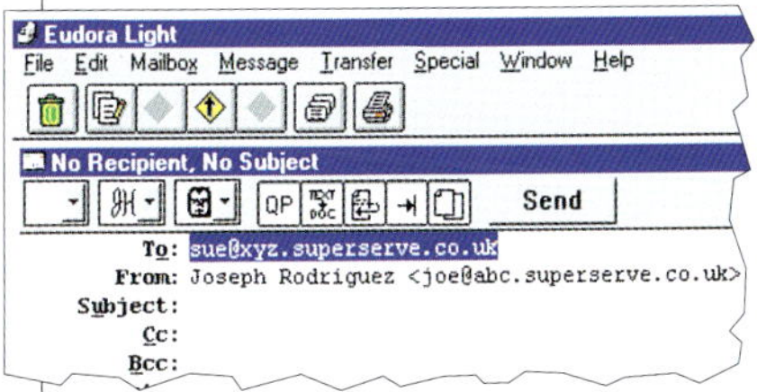


1 △ Highlight outgoing address by holding down mouse button and dragging across full e-mail address.

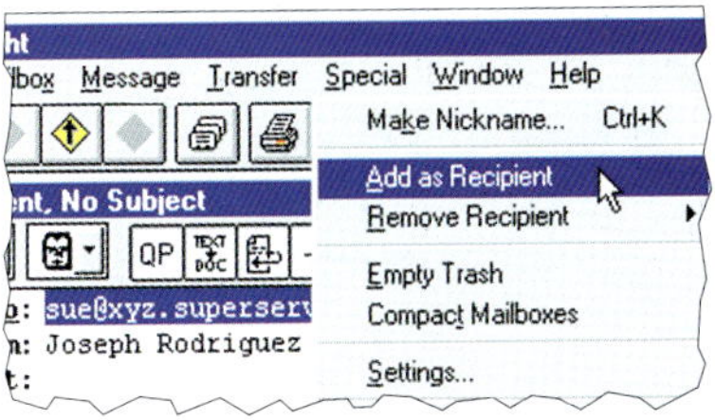


2 △ Choose *Add as Recipient* from *Special* menu and release mouse button. Address is now stored.

3 ▷ Select *New Message To* from *Message* menu. Newly added e-mail address will appear alongside *New Message To*, in drop-down-menu window.

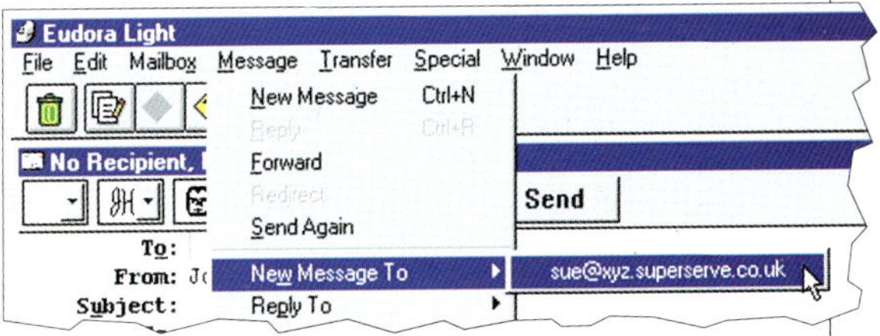


# 36 USING ELECTRONIC MAILING LISTS

An electronic mailing list is a database of people who share an interest in a particular subject. Subscribers have thousands of different lists to choose from, and are automatically sent regular information by e-mail about their chosen subject. Each mailing list is managed by a remote computer, known as a listserver, which maintains a list of all users and their addresses, as well as receiving and passing on all e-mail messages contributed to the group.

DATABASE

# DOWNLOADING FILES

## 37 USING FTP TO RETRIEVE OR SEND FILES

Using a process called File Transfer Protocol (FTP), you can access any of the millions of files and programs available on the Internet, and transfer them to your hard disk. ("Protocol" refers to a series of standard, predefined messages that allow a file to be retrieved, regardless of the type of computer you use.) To transfer files with FTP, you need a file transfer program on your hard disk: this should have been supplied by your service provider.

△ FTP VIA A WEB BROWSER

FTP CLIENT PROGRAM ▽

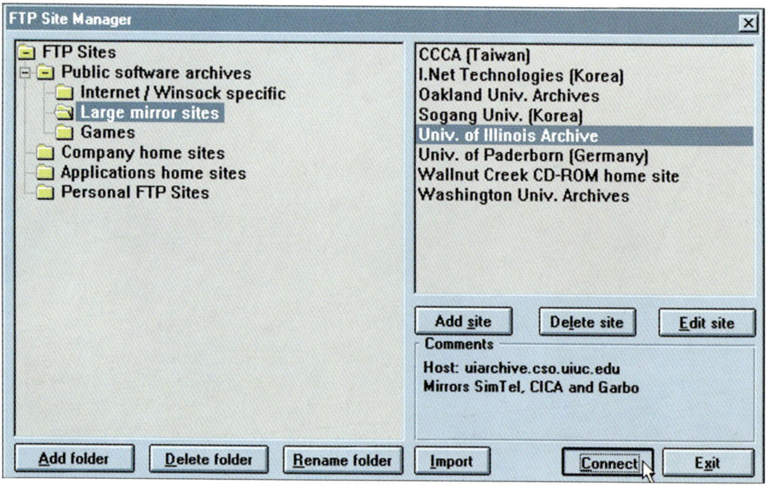

# 38 WHAT IS STORED IN FILES?

The Internet is a huge source of information that is accessible to individual subscribers across the globe. Any kind of information that can be stored on a computer – by individuals, educational or research establishments, governments, or by commercial organizations – is available: the quantity and range are almost beyond comprehension.

***Documents abound*** *in enormous quantities. The Gutenberg Project archive (at* **uiarchive.cso.uiuc.edu/pub/etex/gutenberg**)*, for example, holds thousands of complete electronic texts from* Aesop's Fables *to* Zen and the Art of the Internet.

***Software of almost any type*** *is freely available for you to try out or even use indefinitely. For example, you can download many* Windows 95 *drivers and updates from* **ftp.microsoft.com**.

***Music, sounds, and speech*** *of all descriptions are available from FTP sites. For a collection of sound clips from the Star Trek TV series, for example, visit* **ftp.cc.umanitoba.ca**.

***Nearly every kind of image*** *is available on FTP sites, including photographs and video. For example, there is a wonderful collection of NASA space photographs at* **explorer.arc.nasa.gov/pub/SPACE**.

## 39 HOW DO YOU KNOW WHERE TO LOOK?

One of the biggest problems with FTP is finding out what is actually available and where to access it. One approach is to use a database of FTP sites called Archie, which you can access via the Web at **http://archie.internic.net**. (This is only one of dozens of Archie servers around the world.) You can then instigate a search by typing in all or part of the name of the file or the program. You can also access Archie using dedicated client software such as *WSArchie*.

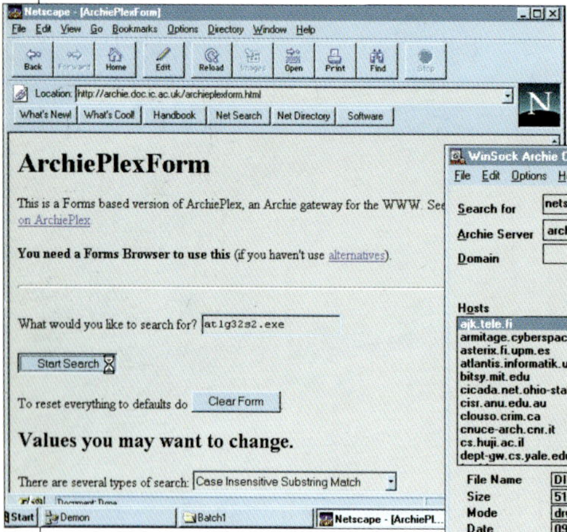


◁ WEB SEARCH
*This screen shows an Archie search using a Web browser –* Netscape Navigator.

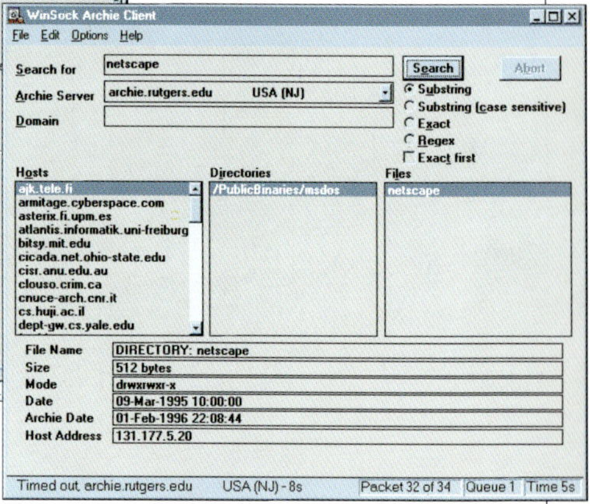


WSARCHIE ▷
*This is a dedicated client program for accessing Archie databases.*

READ THE INSTRUCTIONS
*When you log on to an FTP site, be sure to read the opening screens. Some FTP programs open "readme" screens automatically when you log on; others require you to choose to view them.*

## 40 LOGGING ON TO AN FTP SITE

In order to access an FTP site and transfer files from it to your hard disk, you need an FTP program or a Web browser that supports File Transfer Protocol. Your service provider may have supplied you with an FTP program, but many alternatives are available on the Internet if you would like to experiment.

## 41 CHOOSE AN FTP PROGRAM

Below are listed three of the most popular FTP programs.

- *CuteFTP*: A shareware program providing a number of sites that can be accessed simply from its FTP *Site Manager* window.
- *WS-FTP32*: A freeware program that is easy to use. More information is available on the Web at **http://www.csra.net/junodj/ws_ftp32.htm**.
- *FTP Explorer*: With a similar interface to that of *Windows Explorer*, this program is currently free for noncommercial use and is available at **http://www.windows95.com/apps/ftp.html**.

**WINDOWS® 95 FTP PROGRAM**
*Although more suited to advanced Internet users, the FTP program that is supplied with* Windows 95 *provides a simple command-line interface, where you type UNIX-style commands (similar to those used in Telnet). To run the program, choose* Run *from the* Start *menu and type* **ftp**.

## 42 WHAT IS "FREE" SOFTWARE?

The software that you can access and download from the Internet is freely available but it is not necessarily free. Be sure to check the conditions that apply to any file you download, since some software carries conditions that must be complied with legally. Most software includes a text file providing you with information about the author, the license, and any specific action that you are required to take.

FREE SOFTWARE

### Shareware

- Free to download.
- Free to try for a limited period.
- Protected by copyright.
- After trial period, you must stop using it, or register and pay a fee.

**WHY REGISTER SHAREWARE?**
*Registered versions usually include extra features, such as technical support and free upgrades. Your registration fee also helps fund further product development.*

### Public Domain

- Free to download and use.
- Free from copyright protection.
- May be altered and used for profit.
- Must be explicitly declared as public domain by author; if not, assume that copyright applies.

### Freeware

- Free to download and use.
- You do not need to register it.
- Protected by copyright.

# 43 TRANSFER FILES WITH CUTEFTP

Widely available on the Internet, *CuteFTP* is a shareware FTP program that provides simple access to a number of sites from its *FTP Site Manager* window. It requires no configuration; just install the software on your hard disk, then follow the steps below.

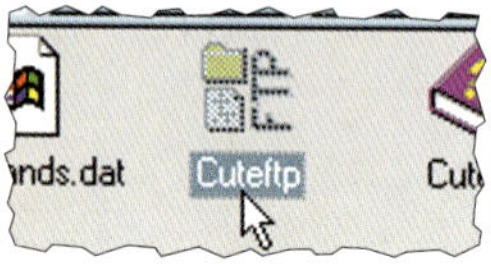


1 △ Double-click *CuteFTP* icon in *CuteFTP* folder. *CuteFTP* window will now open.

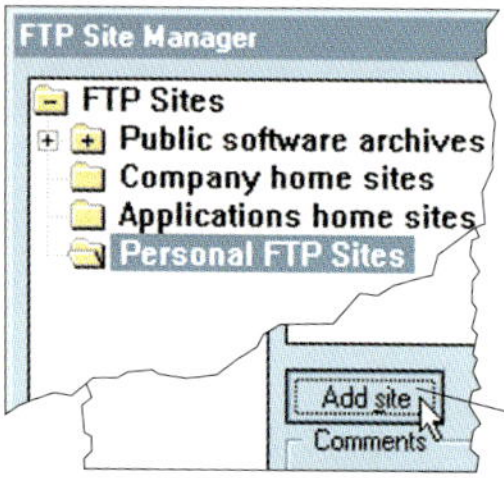


*Click* Add site *button*

2 ◁ *FTP Site Manager* window will also now be open. Click on *Personal FTP Sites*, in left-hand panel, then click *Add site* button.

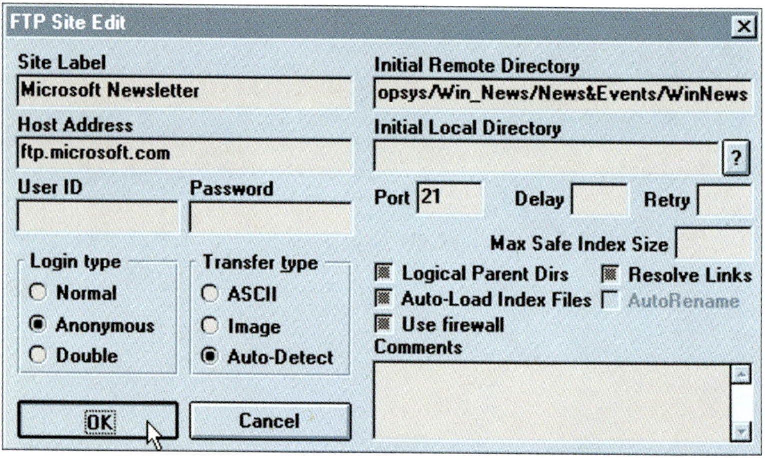


3 △ Identify session by typing description in *Site Label* box. Type site address in *Host Address* box and give additional details of directory you want to access in *Initial Remote Directory* box.

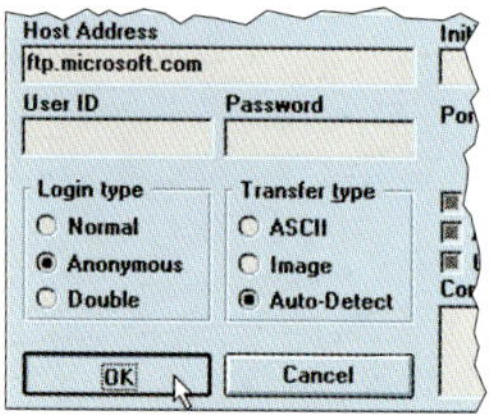


4 ◁ Make sure that box next to *Anonymous* in *Login type* panel and box next to *Auto-Detect* in *Transfer type* panel are checked. Add your e-mail address to *Password* box, and then click *OK*.

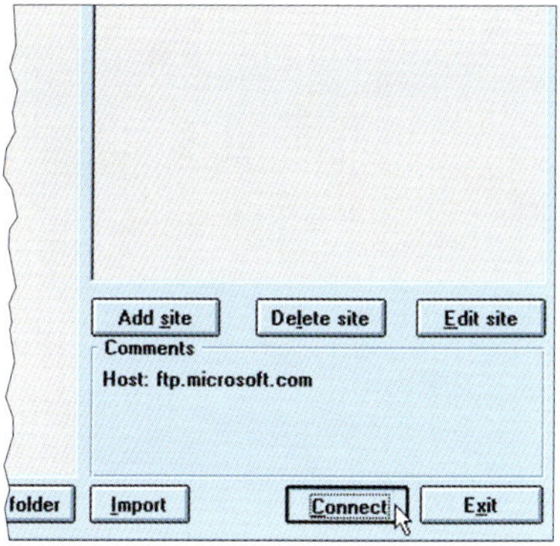


5 △ Session name will appear in *FTP Site Manager* dialog box. Click to highlight it, then click *Connect*.

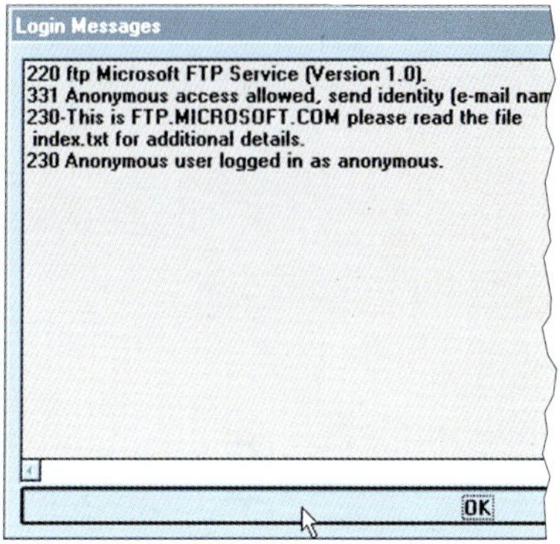


6 △ Read any welcome messages or announcements that appear on screen. Click *OK* to proceed.

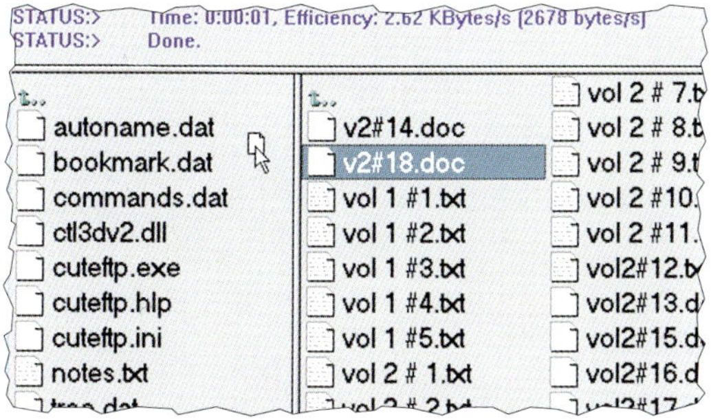


7 ◁ Once you have successfully logged on, directory list for remote site will appear in right-hand panel of *CuteFTP* window. To transfer file from FTP site to your hard disk, click on required file in right-hand panel and drag it over left-hand panel.

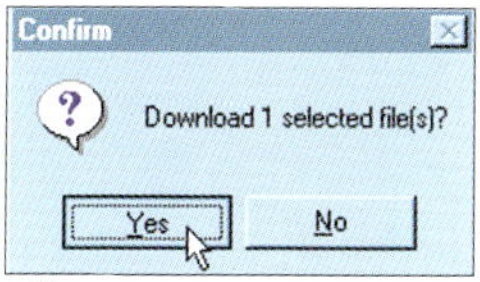


8 △ When *Confirm* dialog box appears, click *Yes* to continue. When file has been successfully transferred, its name will appear in left-hand panel.

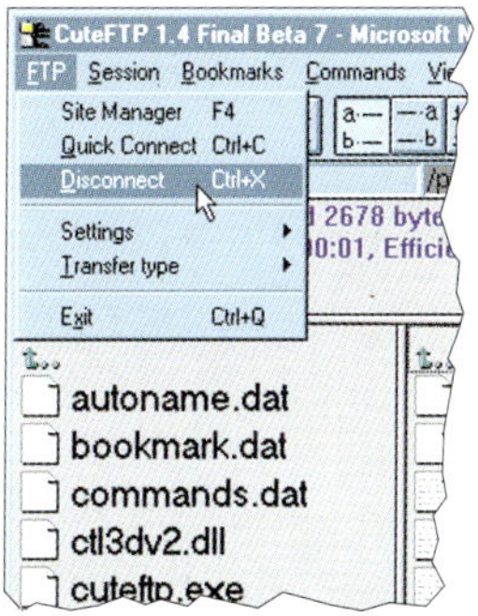


9 ◁ To disconnect from remote site at end of session, choose *Disconnect* from menu in *CuteFTP* window.

CHECK COMPATIBILITY

*Before downloading FTP files, consider whether they are compatible with your computer or require any special hardware.*

## 44 LOGGING ON PROCEDURE

Whichever FTP program you have installed on your computer, you must follow the same basic procedure to log on to an FTP site and must supply the following information:

- Site Address: this can include information about the directories on the site. Use the full address if you know it and if your FTP program allows; otherwise, use the main site address and navigate to the directory you require.
- User Name: when a user name is requested, type **anonymous**.
- Password: when a password is requested, type your e-mail address.

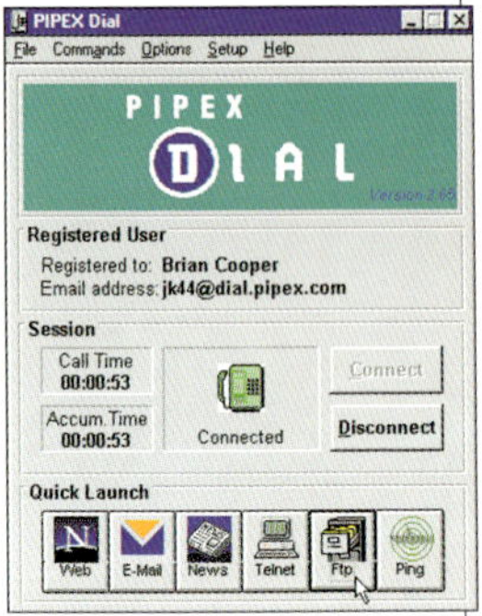


SPEEDY SERVICE
*This Pipex Dial menu has a quick-start FTP button.*

## 45 USING ANONYMOUS FTP

When you want to transfer a file from a remote site, you must first log on to that computer. Most FTP sites simplify the procedure by having a special user account, which can be accessed by anybody. When asked for your user name, simply type in **anonymous**.

## 46 RECOGNIZING FILE TYPES

FTP sites contain numerous different types of files that have different extensions. These tell you, at a glance, what the files contain. Some files may be compressed or encoded and will require special applications to decompress them or make their contents available.

◁ IMAGES
*Common image file extensions are:* jpg, gif, tif, bmp, pcd.

◁ AUDIO
*Among the most common audio file formats are* wav, mid, voc, au.

◁ VIDEO
*Video file extensions include* avi, mov, dl, gr, mpg.

◁ PROGRAMS
*File extensions for application programs include* com, exe, bat.

◁ COMPRESSED FILES
*Extensions used for compressed files include* zip, lzh, gz, Z, zoo, arj.

◁ TEXT
*Common text extensions are* txt, doc, ps, eps, htm, html.

# 47 MOVING AROUND AN FTP SITE

Once you have logged on to an FTP site, you may want to explore the contents or you may be looking for a particular file. In any case, first read any "help," "readme," or "index" files on the server. The illustration below shows how to use *CuteFTP* to access directories and files on an FTP site, but most FTP programs are similar.

△ VIEWING TEXT FILES
*To view text files such as "index," "readme," or "help," highlight file and simply choose* View *from* Commands *menu.*

***To move up** to a higher directory, double-click this symbol. It does not appear when you are in server's top-level (root) directory.*

***The status box** provides information about the status of the current FTP session: for example, the progress of file transfer.*

***Information boxes** show active directories. Here the* download *directory is open on the hard disk and the root directory on the server.*

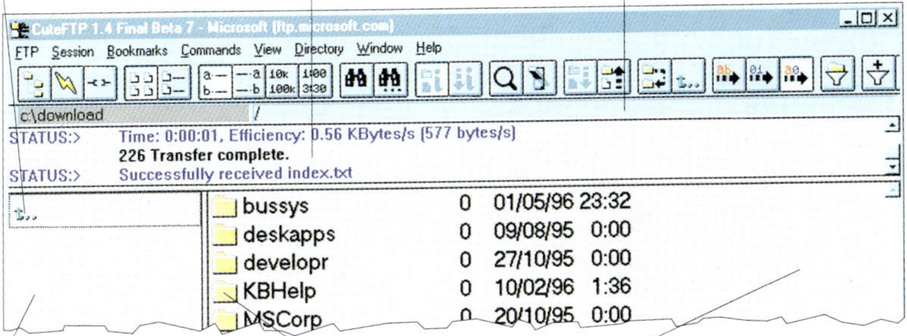


***The left-hand panel** relates to the hard disk. Here, the* download *folder is used to save files transferred from the Internet.*

***To move down a directory** and view the contents, double-click on the selected folder icon in the right-hand panel.*

***The right-hand panel** relates to the FTP server. Navigate to the folder from which you plan to download files to your hard disk.*

# 48 USING ANTIVIRUS PROGRAMS

To protect your computer from viruses, be sure to scan every file that you download with one of the many powerful antivirus programs that are available as freeware and shareware (*Tip 42*) on the Internet.

VIRUS ALERT

# THE WORLD WIDE WEB

## 49 WHAT IS THE WORLD WIDE WEB?

Considered by many users to be the most exciting aspect of the Internet, the World Wide Web is certainly the fastest-growing area, with over 15 million Web pages to visit and thousands more appearing every month.

The Web is a universe of pages containing text, images, sounds, and video clips. Each page is linked to other pages. The Web can also be used to retrieve files and documents from other types of Internet sites.

The Web is based on Hypertext Mark-up Language (HTML). This computer programming language was developed during the 1980s by Tim Berners-Lee, who first had the idea of creating an electronic web of research information.

◁ VERY BEST OF THE WEB
*For an up-to-date directory of the best Web sites, click* Best of the Web *on the start page of* Microsoft Internet Explorer.

*Web of linked documents contains text, images, sounds, video clips, and commercial activity*

## 50 WHAT CAN YOU USE THE WEB FOR?

The pages of the Web cover a vast range of topics, presented in an attractive, interesting, and easily accessible form. The information is interactive, so navigating the Web is similar to using a multimedia CD-ROM – clicking on a "live" area takes you to a new, related screen. Some of the most entertaining Web sites are those run by fans, and whatever your interests, you will find a site somewhere run by a fellow enthusiast.

COMMERCIAL ACTIVITY ▷
*As businesses have recognized the huge customer base that the Web accesses, sites advertising new products or offering home shopping have begun to proliferate.*

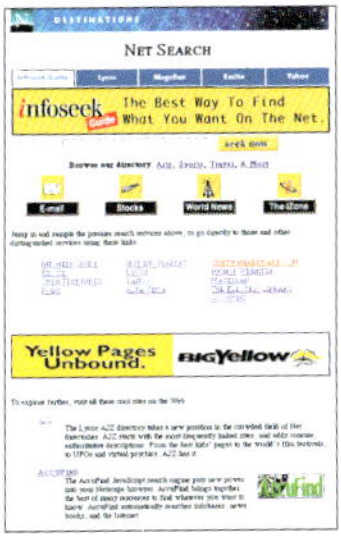


◁ RESEARCH
*Many academic, government, and commercial bodies publish authoritative and reliable material on the Web, making it a very useful tool for anyone involved in research.*

◁ PERSONAL INTERESTS
*Many Web users set up home pages for fun, often providing personal histories and describing their interests. Users can enjoy being part of a global community.*

## 51 E-MAIL VIA THE WEB

If your on-line activity is centered around the Web, you will probably find it convenient to use the e-mail facility in your Web browser. For example, *Netscape Navigator* has its own mail program, which allows you to access the mail window by simply clicking the mail icon in the *Window* menu.

## 52 SURFING THE WEB

It's easy to surf the Web, but you may be daunted by the volume of material available. Netscape's site has two pages that make good starting points for you to get a feel for what is out there: What's New (**http://home.netscape.com/home/whats-new.html**) and What's Cool (**http://home.netscape.com/home/whats-cool.html**).

# 53 WHAT HAPPENS ON A WEB PAGE?

Web pages range from quite simple, text-only, static documents to adventurous sites containing animation, sound, and interactive elements. Many Web pages allow you to download pictures, sounds, and video clips, as well as files and software, and most contain links to related pages on the same or other Web sites. Many pages also contain e-mail addresses, enabling you to contact the producer of the page.

**WHAT IS A TYPICAL WEB PAGE?**

*Although there is no such thing as a typical Web page, the one on the right is a good example of a colorful, well-organized site. It contains textual and graphical links to other pages, a database of recipes, an interactive on-line reference work, and an e-mail facility for sending favorite recipes to your friends.*

*Images, buttons, and icons often provide links to other Web pages or sites. Some images, for example maps, may contain several links. You can usually tell if an image contains a link, since your mouse pointer will change shape when it is moved over a "hot" area.*

*Text with links to other pages is often indicated by being underlined or shown in a different color from the main text.*

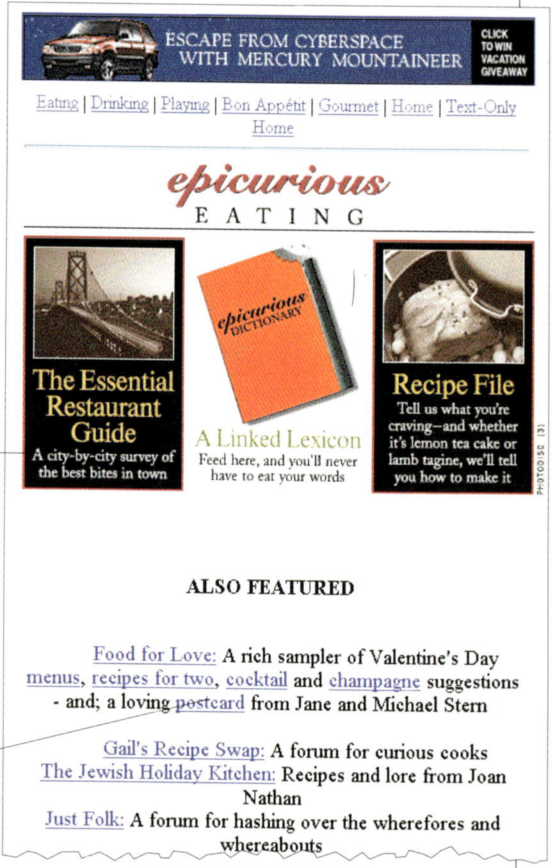


A WELL-ORGANIZED WEB PAGE

## 54 HOW TO IDENTIFY A WEB SITE

A Web site is distinguished by the prefix **http://** in its address. Http, which is short for HyperText Transport Protocol, refers to the standard method of transferring documents that have been created with HyperText Mark-up Language (HTML) between Web servers and browsers. Each Web site has a unique address, known as a URL.

WEB ADDRESSES
*Be careful when you enter Web addresses manually. These never contain spaces and are sensitive to punctuation and case. Some contain capital letters, but they are usually lower case.*

***www** indicates the name of a designated Web server. Although there are many possible variations, it is standard practice to name the Web server "www."*

***/home.html** denotes the directory path on the server. Here the file name is "home," and the final extension indicates that the file is an HTML file.*

***http://** indicates to your browser that you are connecting to a Web document. The letters "http" are always followed by a colon and two forward slashes, as illustrated in this example.*

***.superserve** is the name of the host or domain. This is the commercial organization on whose computer the particular Web page resides.*

***.com** (in this example) indicates that* superserve *is a commercial enterprise. The final suffix, known as the zone name, indicates the nature of the organization.*

## 55 THE ROLE OF HYPERTEXT

The term "hypertext" refers to text containing links to other pieces of text, either within the same document or in another one. Most Web pages are based on HyperText Mark-up Language, which is a set of codes that can be inserted into documents to control the layout and to create links to related topics in other documents.

## 56 WHAT IS A WEB BROWSER?

A Web browser is simply a program that enables a computer to download and view pages of the Web. However, browsers are now developing into sophisticated launchpads for most Internet activities. Two of the most popular versions are *Netscape Navigator* from Netscape Corporation and *Microsoft Internet Explorer*.

***The Address box** displays the URL (Uniform Resource Locator) of the site that is currently open in* Internet Explorer.

***Basic functions** are easy to access from the start page. Access further features from menus and* Options *dialog boxes.*

***Click the Links** button to access a toolbar providing links to support pages and information about new Web sites.*

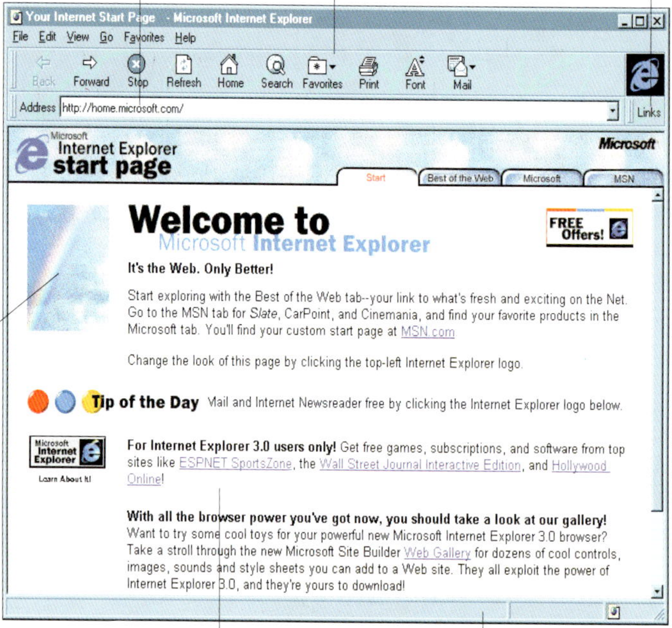


***The main browser** window shows the pages that make up the Web. Colored or underlined text indicates "hot" links.*

***Click tabs** on the home page to access directories of Web sites, information about* Microsoft *and* Internet Explorer, *etc.*

***The status bar** shows information about the current Web page, such as the names of image files being downloaded.*

# 57 CHANGING YOUR OPTIONS

If it is running slowly, you can speed up *Microsoft Internet Explorer* just by changing your options and choosing not to load particular types of files automatically. Choose *Options* from the *View* menu. Now you can choose *not* to display images when viewing a Web page by unchecking the *Show Pictures* box on the *General* page.

HELP THIS WEB BROWSER RUN FASTER ▷

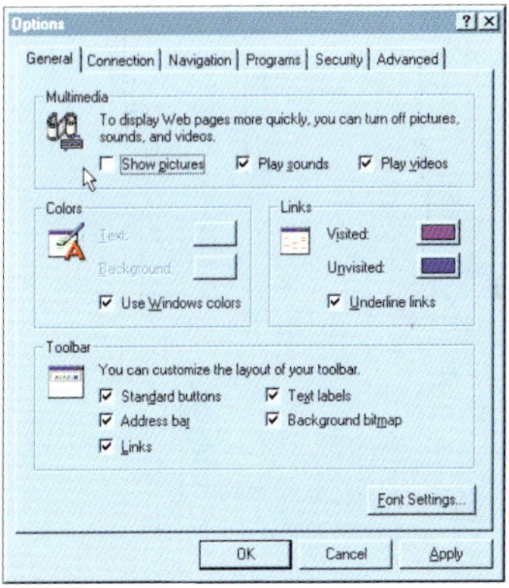


# 58 BOOKMARK YOUR FAVORITE PAGES

During your Web-browsing sessions, you may visit dozens of sites and will need some means of keeping track of those pages to which you intend to return. Most Web browsers include a bookmark feature that you can access quickly and that usually allows you to organize your bookmarks into a hierarchical drop-down menu. In *Microsoft Internet Explorer*, such markers are known as "favorites."

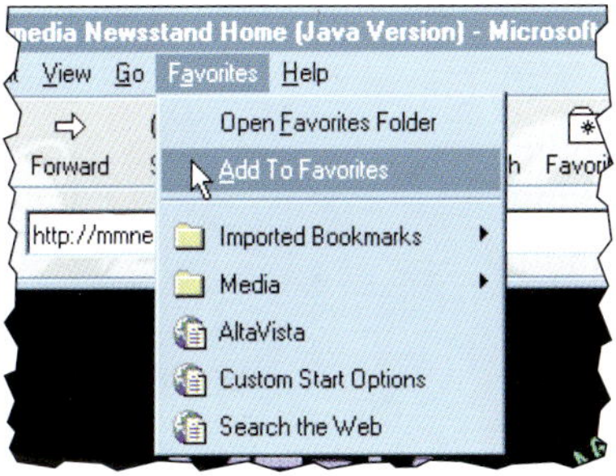


MICROSOFT INTERNET EXPLORER FAVORITES
*Managing "favorites" using* Microsoft Internet Explorer *is similar to managing folders in* Windows 95. *Because you are prompted to file new entries as you create them, minimal management is required.*

NETSCAPE NAVIGATOR BOOKMARKS
*If you keep the* Bookmarks *window open during a Web session, you can manage your bookmarks as you proceed. New entries can be dropped directly into a folder with the* Quick Link *feature.*

# 59 MULTIMEDIA ON THE WEB

The latest technologies have transformed Web pages from static pages to multimedia creations of sound, movement, and interactive links that you can access from a Web browser. All browsers can display HTML-formatted text and most image files, but the latest versions of *Netscape Navigator* and *Microsoft Internet Explorer* can also automatically handle a number of audio, video, and 3-D file formats. Browsers can be enhanced to handle additional file types by downloading and installing browser plug-ins (*Tip 60*).

△ STREAMED SOUND

*Many pages contain "streamed" sound files that you can listen to as they download. The* Independent Underground Music Archive *at* **http://www.iuma.com** *offers sound files in several formats, for example.*

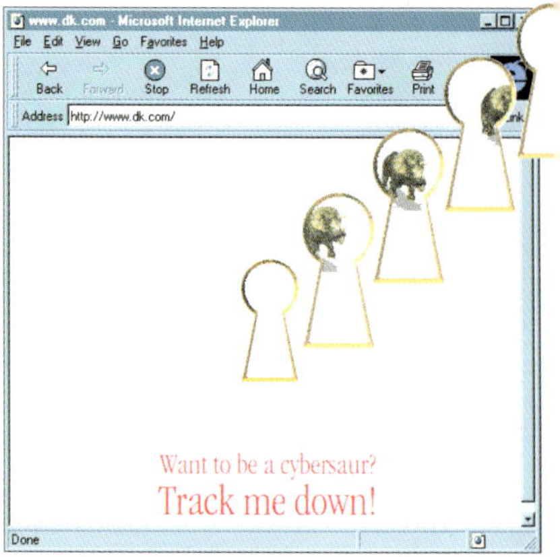


△ ANIMATED SEQUENCE

*This sequence (on Dorling Kindersley's Web site at* **http://www.dk.com**) *was produced using the animated GIF (GIF 89a) format. The latest browsers need no additional plug-ins to handle this file type.*

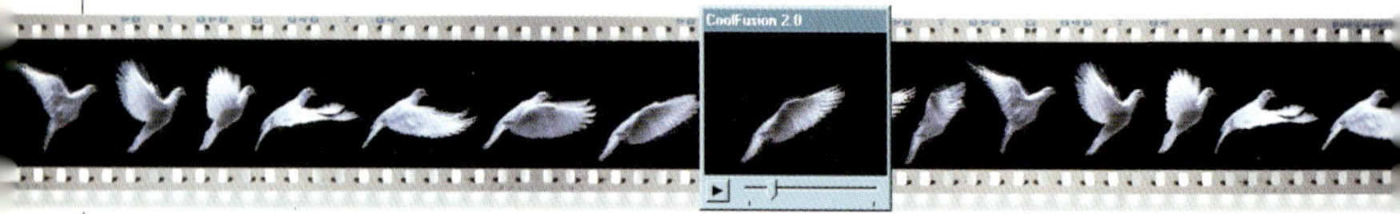


△ STREAMED VIDEO

*Some of the newer Web browsers handle streamed video by playing a little at a time as it is received over the Internet.*

*This clip from the multimedia showcase at* **http://www.wintermute.net/pic.html** *is displayed using* CoolFusion *– a plug-in preinstalled on* Netscape Navigator.

*Separate images* are cycled to give the appearance of animation.

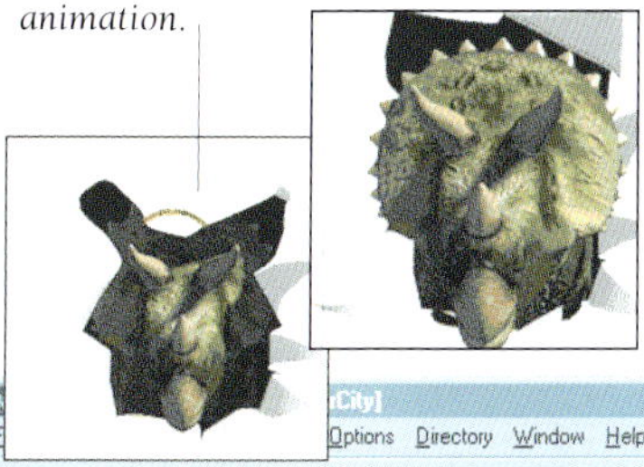

**WHAT IS JAVA?**
*Java is a programming language that enables Web pages to contain miniature programs (known as applets) that appear as animation, sound, scrolling text, or interactive features. In order to view JAVA applets, your Web browser must be JAVA-enhanced.*

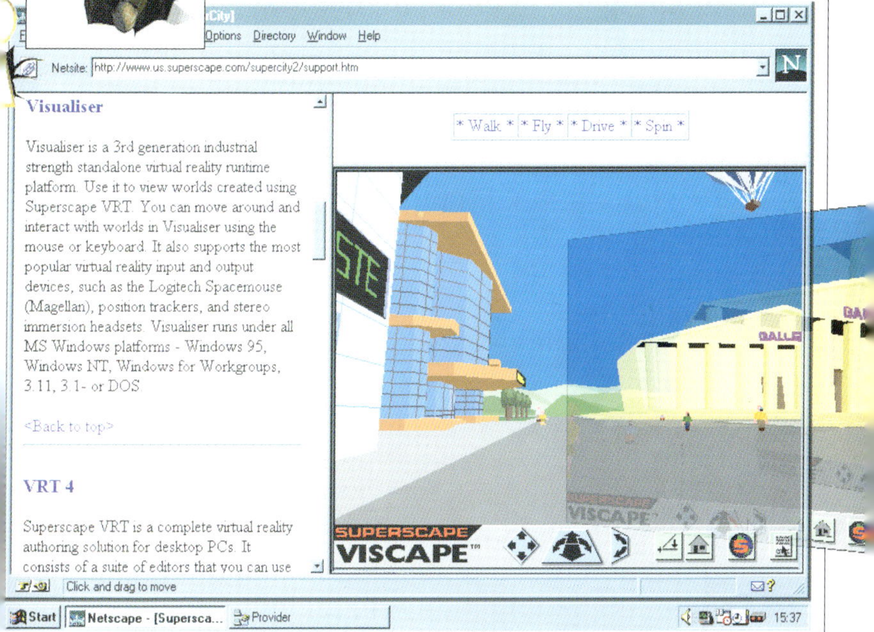


△ THREE-DIMENSIONAL GRAPHICS
*A VRML (Virtual Reality Modeling Language) program enables you to explore virtual worlds and manipulate three-dimensional images on the Net. This example shows Viscape, by Superscape, which you can download from* http://www.superscape.com.

△ NAVIGATING IN 3-D
*The controls at the bottom of the window allow you to travel around the screen and offer a 360° range of movement.*

# 60 WHAT ARE PLUG-INS?

A plug-in is a program that adds features to a Web browser so that it can handle files containing different elements, such as 3-D and multimedia. You can download new plug-ins and upgrades for existing ones, usually from the software developer's home page. Keep in touch with new developments by visiting one of the regularly updated plug-in lists on the Web.

PREINSTALLED PLUG-INS
*The latest versions of* Netscape Navigator *and* Microsoft Internet Explorer *come with some preinstalled plug-ins.* Internet Explorer *offers a movie player called* ActiveMovie, *for example.*

AUDIO & VIDEO

***Crescendo***
*A free plug-in from LiveUpdate that allows you to play stereo MIDI music from the Web, with a CD-like control panel and digital counter.*

***IntervuMPEG Player***
*Intervu's plug-in lets you play MPEG audio-video files that are streamed as you download them. You can preview the first frame before downloading it.*

***RapidTransit***
*Eastman's* RapidTransit *decompresses and plays high-quality stereo sound from Web pages.*

3D & ANIMATION

***CosmoPlayer***
*Produced by Silicon Graphics,* CosmoPlayer *is a VRML viewer.*

***FutureSplash***
*Use Futurewave's* FutureSplash *to view animated graphics and drawings from the Web.*

***VRScout***
*Chaco Communications' plug-in enables you to interact with 3-D objects and graphic locations.*

***Wirl Virtual Reality Browser***
*This is an advanced VRML plug-in from Vream.*

OTHER PLUG-INS

***Earthtime***
*Starfish Software's plug-in lets you view the time around the world. The animated map indicates daylight and darkness.*

***FIGleaf***
*Produced by Carberry Technology,* FIGleaf *lets your browser view a wide variety of graphic formats (including gif, jpg, png, cgm, and tiff).*

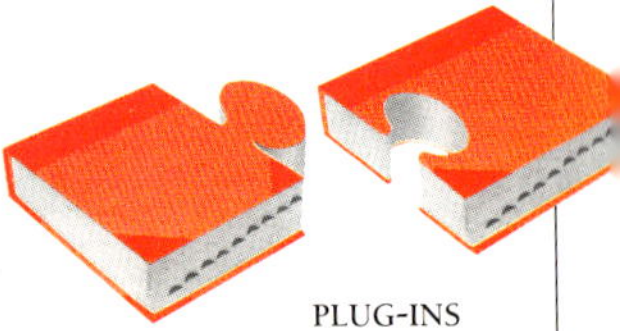

PLUG-INS

# 61 SEARCHING THE WEB

The possibility of finding exactly what you are looking for among the millions of individual Web pages might appear unlikely. However, powerful search tools are available that will trawl Web sites, Gopher sites (*Tips 64 & 65*), and newsgroups, searching for your chosen criteria, and return results within seconds. The two main types of search tool are search engines and Web directories.

# 62 Using the AltaVista Search Engine

*AltaVista* is one of the most popular search engines. To use it, open your Web browser (in this case *Netscape Navigator*) and type the address **http://altavista.digital.com**.

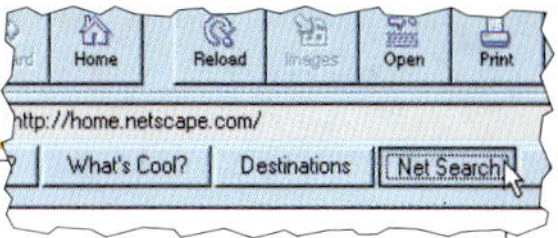


1 △ Click *Net Search* button to take you to all-in-one search page. Each time you click *Net Search* button, *Netscape Navigator* provides entry screen to search engine or Web directory.

2 ◁ From list of search services, click on *AltaVista* to connect to *AltaVista* home page.

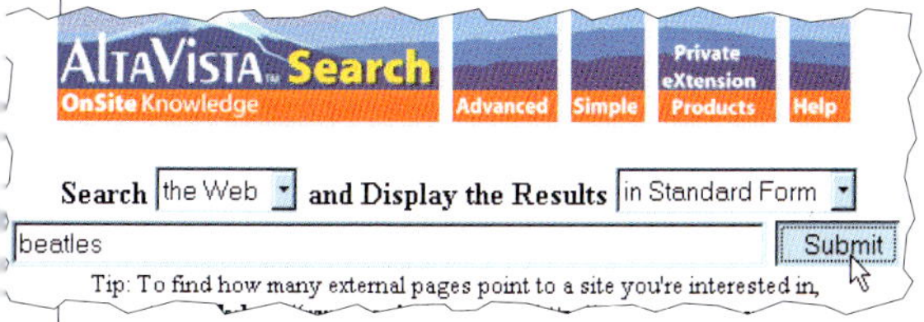


3 ◁ Type subject of search (in this case, Beatles) in criteria box, below *Search*; click *Submit* button.

4 ▷ *AltaVista* tells you how many sites were found, listing first ten in window. To visit any of these, right-click on page title or address; choose *Open in New Window*.

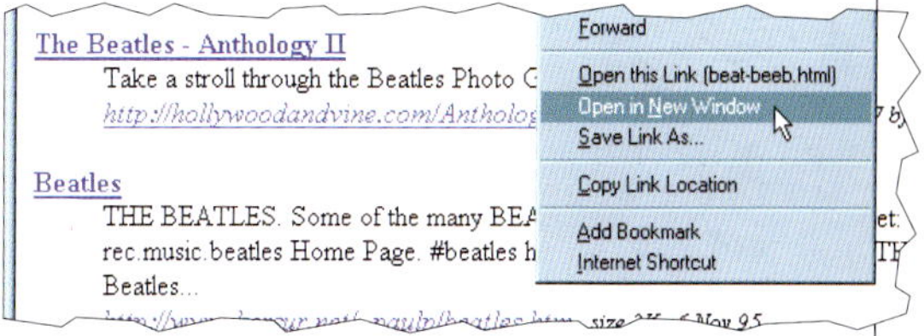


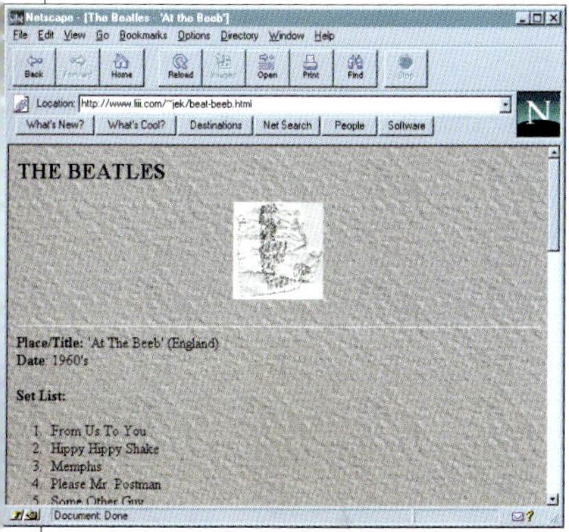


5 ◁ After viewing page, close Web browser window. You can now return to *AltaVista* page displayed in first browser window.

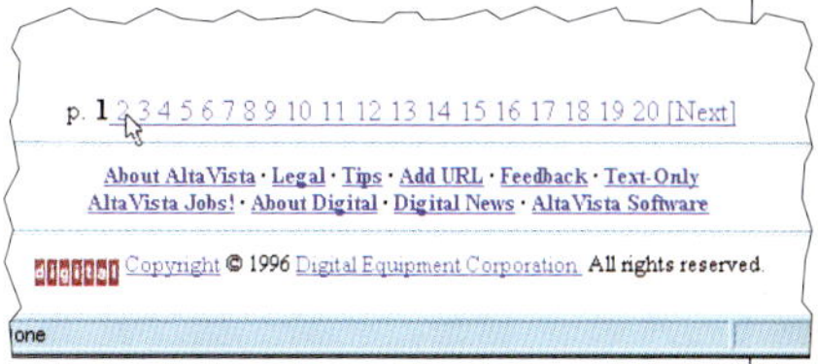


6 △ To look at next page of ten sites relating to your search criterion, scroll to bottom of screen. Click on 2.

## 63 ALL-IN-ONE SEARCH PAGES

A search page provides a direct link to many of the major search engines and directories. Two of the best are provided by Netscape at **http://www.netscape.com/home/internet-search.html** and by Microsoft at **http://www.msn.com/access/allinone.asp**.

## 64 WHAT IS GOPHERSPACE?

Gopher is an information retrieval system that provides access to a huge number of servers (known collectively as Gopherspace). Most of these are maintained by universities or government bodies and hold specialized information that is unlikely to be found on Web sites. Information is presented in menus containing files and folders, known as Gopher holes. You can usually view or download files simply by clicking on them.

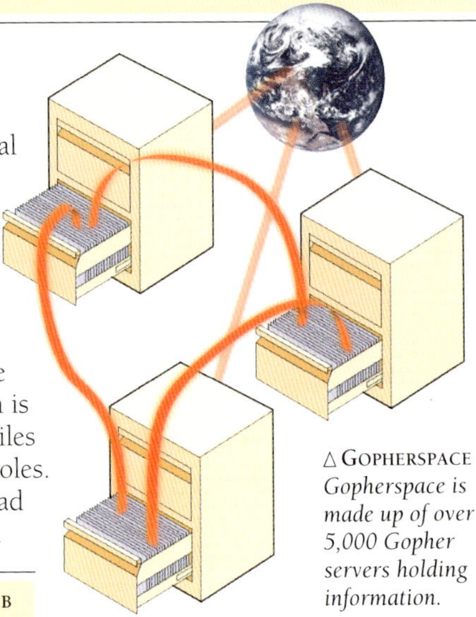

△ GOPHERSPACE
*Gopherspace is made up of over 5,000 Gopher servers holding information.*

CONNECTING TO GOPHER VIA THE WEB
*Originally, Gopherspace could be accessed only with a Gopher client program, but now most users access Gopher sites from a Web browser, prefixing the URL with* **gopher://**

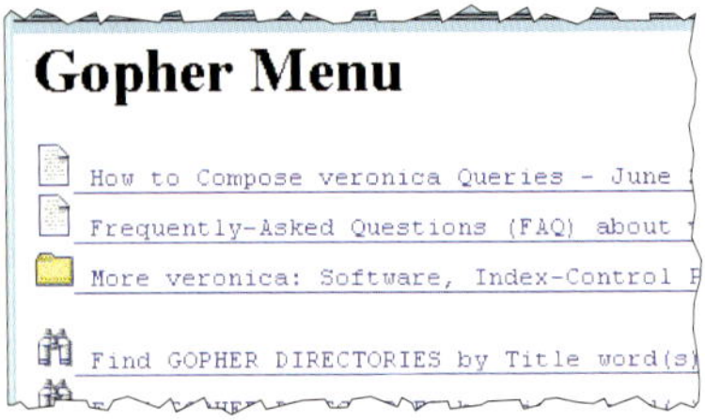


△ SEARCH GOPHERSPACE WITH VERONICA

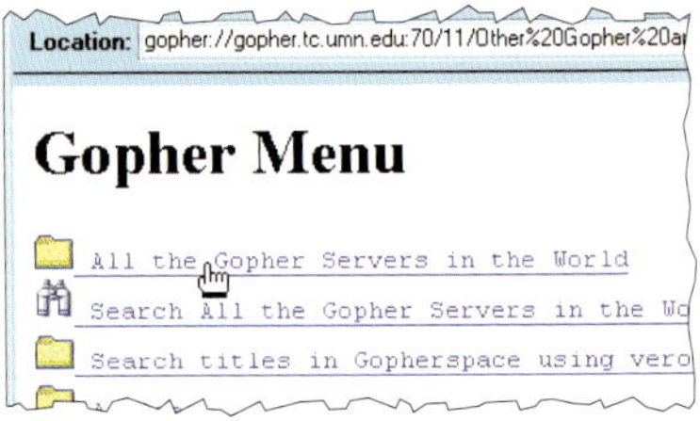


△ VIEW GLOBAL LIST OF GOPHER SERVERS

OTHER GOPHER SERVERS
*These examples show how to use Gopher Menus to find links to other servers and to search Gopherspace. (Veronica is a database of all the files in Gopherspace.)*

# 65 SEARCH GOPHERSPACE WITH VERONICA

The best way to find specific information in Gopherspace is by using a special search tool such as Veronica, which can be run from most Gopher sites. Veronica will search a wide range of files, including text files, images, and programs. The steps here show how to perform a Veronica search from a Web browser.

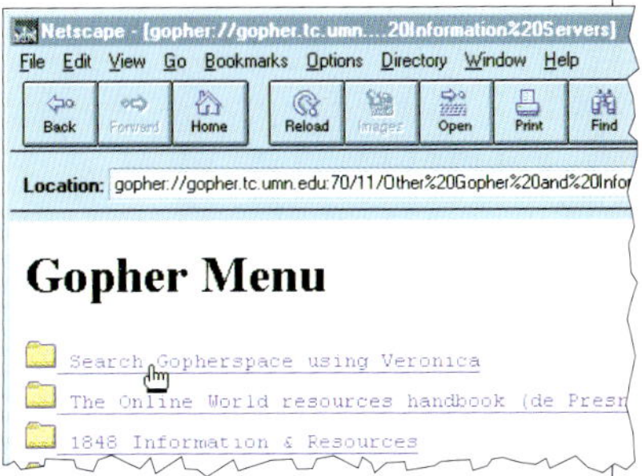


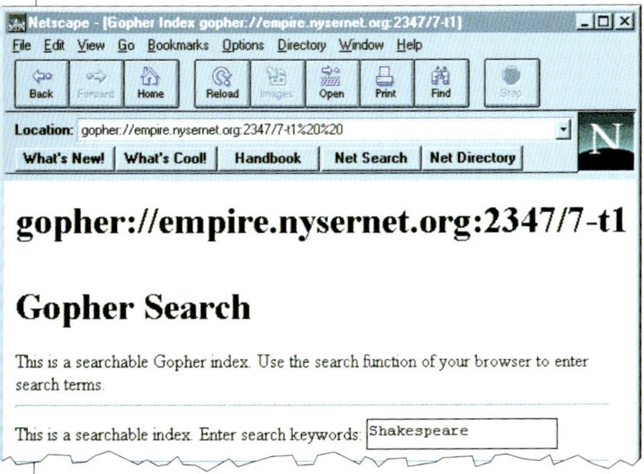


1 △ First, connect to Gopher site by typing **gopher://** followed by name of Gopher site in Web browser's location box. Press Return key, then click Veronica entry in Gopher Menu that appears.

2 ◁ On *Gopher Search* page, type search term in keywords box (here, Shakespeare) and press Return key.

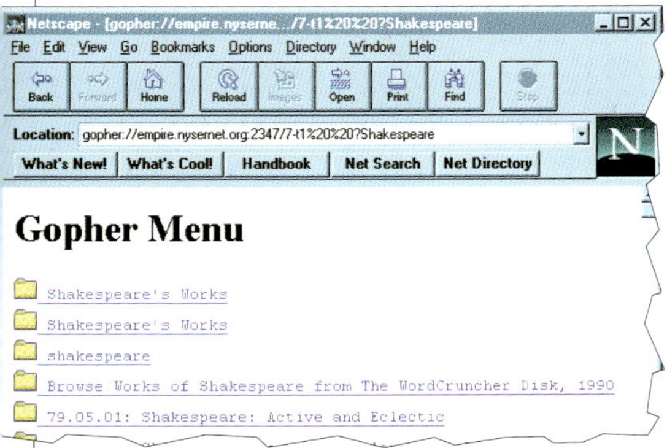


3 ◁ When list of "hits" appears, click on any line in order to move to appropriate file or link on that Gopher site.

**WHY USE VERONICA?**
*Veronica maintains comprehensive databases of all the information in Gopherspace, which can be searched for keywords or individual file names.*

# LOGGING ON WITH TELNET

## 66 UNDERSTANDING TELNET

One of the oldest Internet activities, Telnet is a program that allows you to log on to a remote computer and access services there from your computer. Not all Telnet sites are free, but some research organizations, universities, and libraries offer free access. You control a Telnet session from your keyboard, choosing options from a list, and typing a number or a letter to access a series of menu screens – a little like using an old-fashioned terminal at a public library.

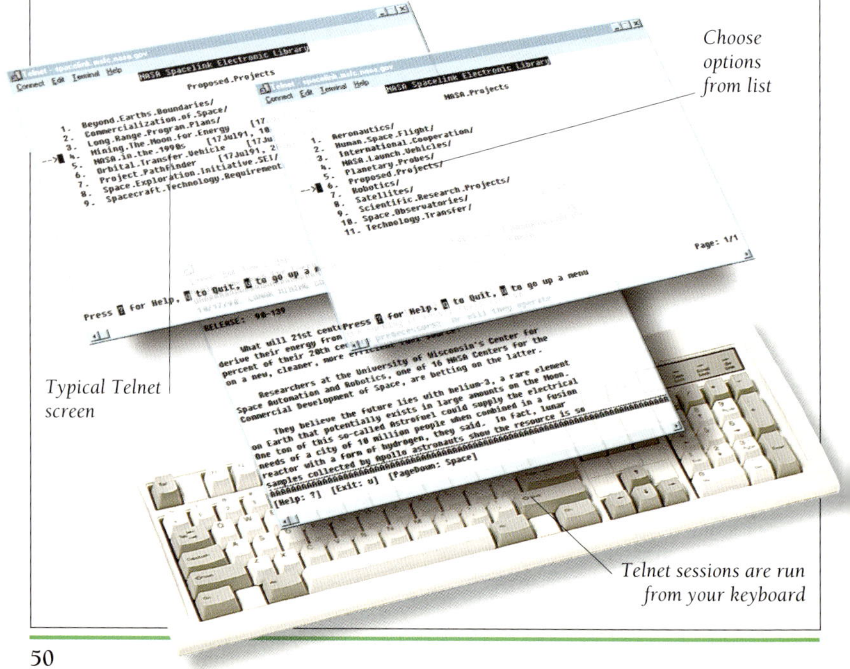


*Choose options from list*

*Typical Telnet screen*

*Telnet sessions are run from your keyboard*

# 67 ACCESSING TELNET WITH WINDOWS® 95

You can access Telnet in two main ways – using *Windows 95* or via the Web – but in either case, you will need to install Telnet software on your computer. It is supplied with *Windows 95* or can be downloaded from an Internet software site such as **http://www.windows95.com**. To log on with *Windows 95*, first double-click on the Telnet icon in the *Windows* folder.

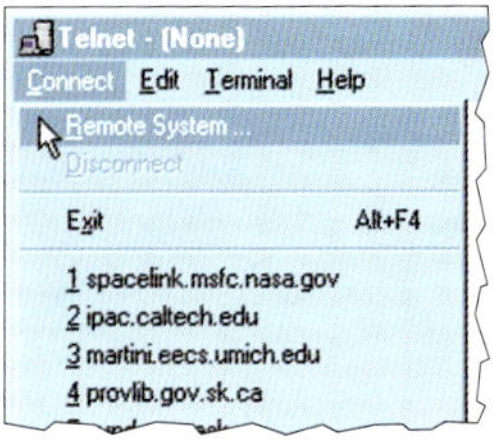


1 △ To access *Connect* box, choose *Remote System* from *Connect*.

USING TELNET
*Most people use Telnet to access on-line databases or to read articles and books on-line. It is also possible to use Telnet to play on-line games and to run other programs. The examples shown are from NASA's Spacelink site at* **spacelink.msfc. nasa.gov**.

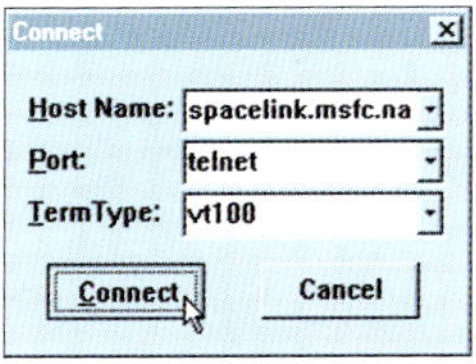


2 ◁ Type name of site you want to access in *Host Name* panel of *Connect* box, then click *Connect* button. When you are connected to site, login screen will appear.

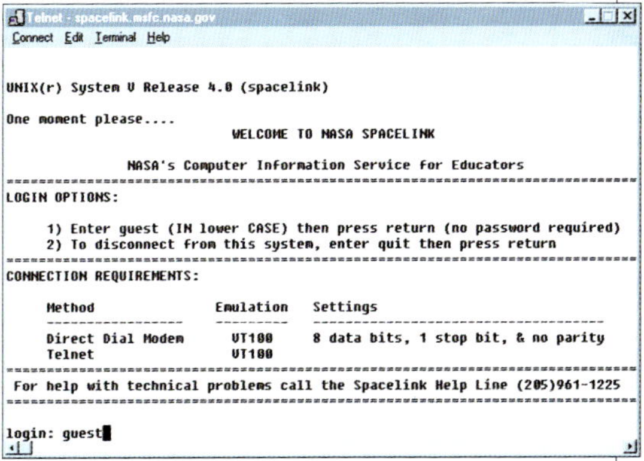


3 ▷ Once connected, follow on-screen instructions. In this example, type **guest** for your login name, as specified, and press Return key. Follow instructions to access further information.

# 68 CAN'T FIND WINDOWS® 95 TELNET PROGRAM?

Access *Find* utility from *Start* menu, choose *Files or Folders*, type **Telnet** in *Named* box, and click *OK*. Right-click on Telnet icon when it appears and drag on to desktop. Release mouse button over desktop and choose *Create Shortcut(s)* from menu that appears.

## 69 ACCESSING TELNET WITH A WEB BROWSER

As well as using *Windows 95* to access Telnet, you can configure your Web browser to launch your Telnet client automatically when you click on a link to a Telnet site or when you type in a URL starting **telnet://**. To configure *Netscape Navigator*, for example, follow the steps below, and the next time you access a Telnet site, the Telnet software will be launched automatically.

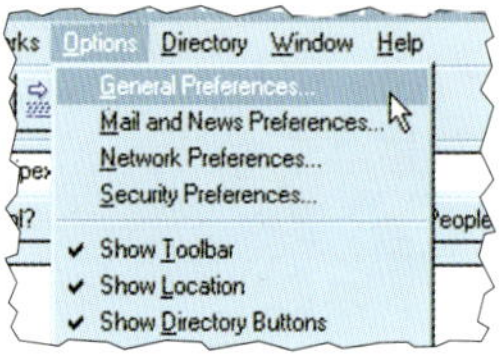


1 △ From *Options* menu in main *Navigator* window, choose *General Preferences. Preferences* dialog box will appear.

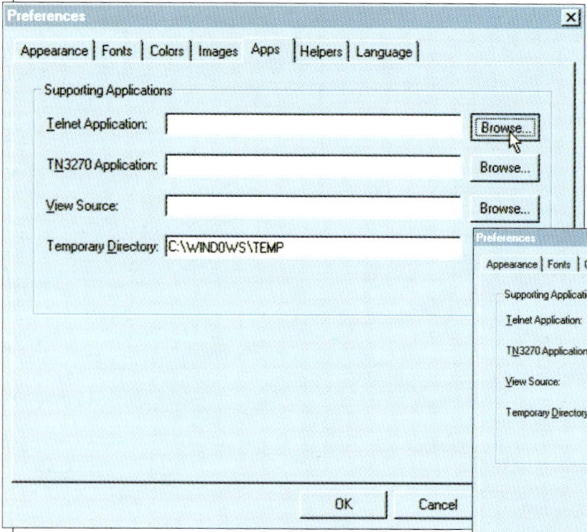


2 ◁ Click *Browse* button on *Apps* page; navigate to your Telnet program in *Select a Telnet Application* window. Click on Telnet application and choose *Open*.

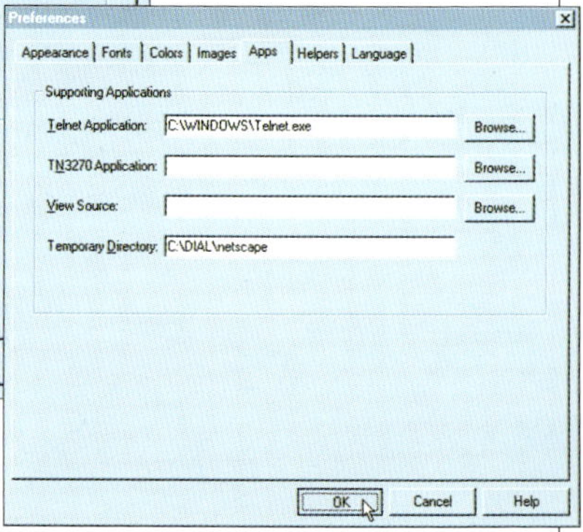


3 ▷ Path for application will now appear in *Telnet Application* box. Finally, click *OK* in *Preferences* box.

## 70 READ THE INSTRUCTIONS

Telnet sites are not all organized in the same way, so it is important to read very carefully the instructions in the opening menu screens when you log on. If you are experiencing difficulties, you can usually call up a help menu by typing **H** or **?** or **help** at any time. If you are really stuck, type **exit** or **logout** to end the session.

# NEWSGROUPS ON THE INTERNET

## 71 WHAT ARE NEWSGROUPS?

Newsgroups on the Internet have little to do with "news," but instead provide a unique opportunity for public discussion and debate. Participants "post" messages that are available to all readers of the newsgroup, who can then choose to reply – either publicly or privately – to the message. The messages can include sounds, images, or video clips. Newsgroups thus provide a forum for interested parties to discuss topics of mutual interest, and offer some of the most stimulating content on the Internet.

POSTED MESSAGES

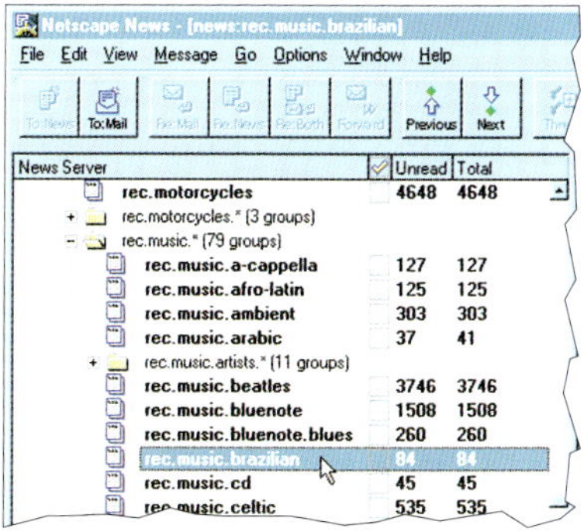


△ NETSCAPE NEWSREADER
*The* Netscape Navigator *Web browser has a built-in newsreader that makes it easy to access newsgroups.*

## 72 THE USENET NETWORK

Usenet is the name given to the huge body of newsgroups that are distributed around the world by computers known as "news servers." These servers exchange information so that each one carries a copy of the most recent messages. Usenet is not part of the Internet, although Internet sites are used to carry its newsgroups. If you are not linked to the Internet, you can still access newsgroups by dialing a BBS that carries Usenet.

## 73 NEWSGROUP CLASSIFICATIONS

Newsgroups in the Usenet network are classified according to subject, with about 20 top-level (major subject) categories. Names of newsgroups, like e-mail addresses, follow a hierarchical structure, with the prefix indicating the top-level classification category.

◁ NEWS
*Look here first if you are new to Usenet. Over 20 groups dealing with the network, including useful software, new groups, and advice. Try* **news.announce.newuser**

COMP ▷
*Over 750 computer-oriented groups, including technical advice. Try* **comp.sys.ibm.pc.games.adventure**

▽ ALT
*Over 2,500 "alternative" groups discussing everything from New Age remedies to independent music. Try* **alt.astrology** *or* **alt.music.beatles**

MISC ▷
*Over 100 assorted groups ranging from pension funds to bodybuilding. Try* **misc.invest.stocks**

△ BIZ
*Over 60 business groups, where marketing and advertising are acceptable activities. Try* **biz.jobs.offered** *or* **biz.comp.services**

◁ REC
*Over 550 groups devoted to recreational activities, including most of the arts. Try* **rec.sport.triathlon**

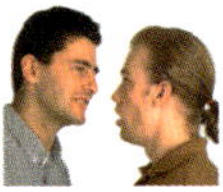

TALK ▷
*More than 20 newsgroups that provide a forum for debate on any topic, especially the more controversial ones. Try* **talk.euthanasia**

▽ SOC
*More than 200 groups concerned with a variety of social, cultural, and religious issues, including the environment, politics, and socializing. Try* **soc.rights.human**

SCI ▷
*Over 150 groups interested in scientific debate and research and development. Try* **sci.virtual=worlds**

## 74 NEWSGROUPS OUTSIDE USENET

There are some newsgroups outside the Usenet umbrella, but they tend to be concerned mainly with local issues. For example, some service providers set up their own local newsgroups in order to enable their subscribers to share information about the service, but these groups are not necessarily distributed to other news servers.

# 75 SETTING UP FREE AGENT

In order to access news groups on your provider's server, you need to install a newsreader program. There are several to choose from: many are available as freeware. *Free Agent* is one of the more comprehensive newsreading programs, allowing a high degree of flexibility. It can be found at **http://www.webpress.net/forte/agent/index.htm**. *Free Agent* will be downloaded as a compressed file and, before you use it, you will have to expand it, using a suitable expansion program such as *WinZip* or *Stuffit Expander*.

1 ◁ Double-click *Agent* icon to start *Free Agent* newsreader.

2 ◁ Type news server's name in *News (NNTP) Server* box, and name of mail server in *Mail (SMTP) Server* box. (Your service provider should have given you this information.) Type your e-mail address in *Email Address* box.

3 ▷ Click on arrow to right of *Time Zone* box and choose correct zone for your town or city from drop-down menu. Click *OK*.

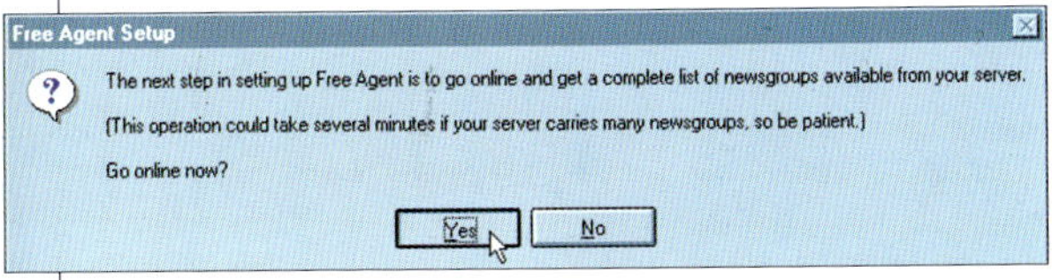


4 ◁ Click *Yes* in dialog box to download list of newsgroups carried by your provider. This may take time.

5 ▷ When *Free Agent* has downloaded full list of newsgroups, they will appear in *All Groups* panel. Use scroll bar on right of panel to browse through list.

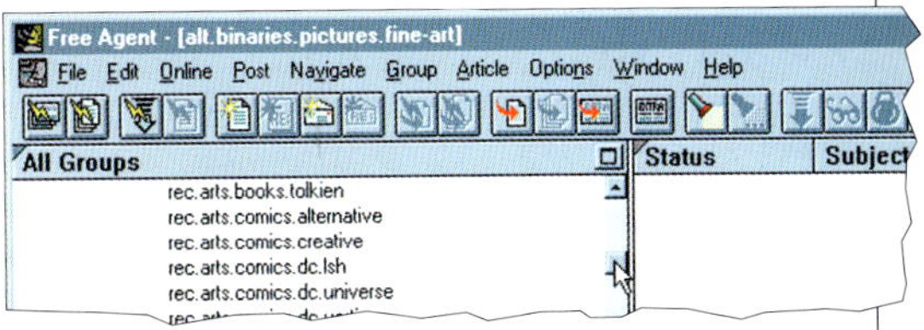

## 76 POSTING MESSAGES

Messages (sometimes known as articles) sent to a newsgroup are said to be "posted," since they address the group rather than an individual. There are various ways of doing this. In these steps you can see how to follow up a newsgroup message that you are currently reading, using the newsreader *Free Agent.*

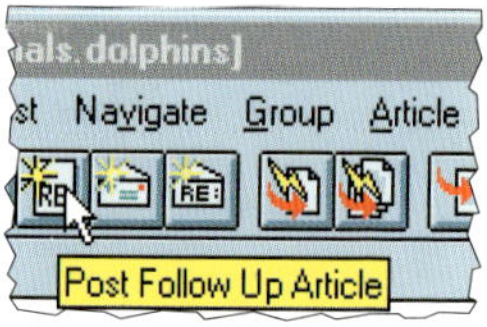


1 △ Click *Post Follow Up Article* button. Mail window with original message and address of group will appear.

2 ◁ In *Email To* box, type address of person whose message you are responding to. This will appear at top of *Text* box.

3 ▷ If necessary, edit original message to include only points you are responding to. Type your follow-up message in *Text* window.

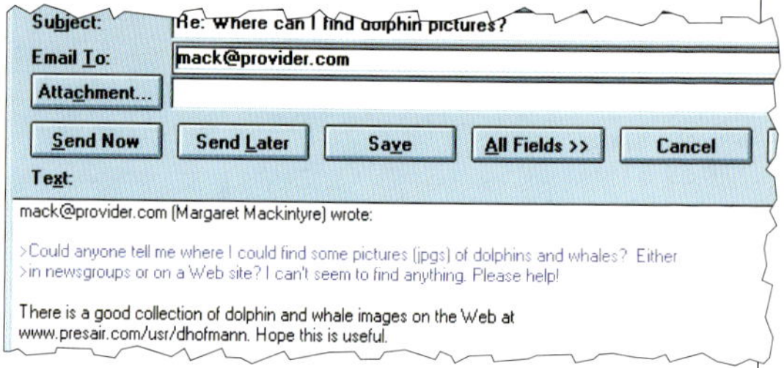


**CENSORING MATERIAL**

*If you are concerned about children accessing unsuitable material, seek advice from your service provider or dealer about software for blocking such information.*

4 ◁ Click *Send Now* button. Message will be posted to newsgroup, and e-mail will be sent to author of message you are responding to.

## 77 REPLYING PRIVATELY TO A MESSAGE

It is considered courteous to reply personally (by sending an e-mail) as well as publicly to the author of a message that has been posted to a newsgroup. However, if you prefer to reply only privately, you can do this by sending an e-mail directly to that person.

## 78 HOW TO BEHAVE IN NEWSGROUPS

Although there are no hard-and-fast rules about how to behave in newsgroups, a voluntary code has grown up with the Usenet network. If you are a newcomer, try to familiarize yourself with these guidelines in order to avoid irritating regular users by barging into discussion without preparation or by posting irrelevant questions.

**LURKING**
*"Lurk" in a newsgroup for a few days before joining so you can find out what the group's concerns are, whether they interest you, and the level at which postings should be aimed.*

## 79 NEWSGROUP NETIQUETTE

The basic principle behind newsgroup netiquette is simply to maintain an awareness of other members of the Usenet and their needs. Bear this in mind and your experiences should be enjoyable.

- **Read the FAQ**
Many newsgroups produce a document containing answers to Frequently Asked Questions. Read this to avoid troubling the group with basic questions.

- **Be Relevant**
Newsgroups often deal with a narrow range of issues, so make sure that your message is relevant.

- **Be Descriptive**
Give your posting a descriptive title to help members choose which articles to read.

- **Be Careful with Humor**
Humor and irony are difficult to convey in written communication so back up ambiguous statements with an "emoticon" (an emotional icon).

- **Avoid "Spamming"**
Posting identical messages to many groups (known as spamming) is frowned upon and may invoke rough justice. For example, spammers may find themselves mail-bombed by thousands of pieces of junk e-mail.

- **Don't be Rude**
If you are irritated by a posting, send a private e-mail rather than conduct an argument in public.

- **Be Brief**
Express yourself in a clear manner and keep your posting concise.

GOOD CONDUCT

# ON-LINE CHATTING

## 80 WHAT IS INTERNET RELAY CHAT?

Developed in 1988, IRC is a system that allows many people to communicate simultaneously on the Internet. Conversations are conducted by typing messages at the keyboard and take place in channels. To take part in IRC, you need to run an IRC client program on your computer while you are connected to the Internet.

COMMUNICATING FROM THE KEYBOARD

**WHERE DO YOU BEGIN?**
*For useful background information, read the IRC FAQs and Primers (find them by running a search for "IRC" on the Web). Try monitoring the newsgroups* alt.irc *and* alt.irc.help *for more help. When you think you are ready, join the* #newbies *or* #ircnewbies *channels: these will help you find your feet without feeling intimidated.*

## 81 CHOOSING AN IRC NETWORK

There are about 15 different networks hosting IRC, and each one exists independently of the others. Since no two networks have the same set of channels available, be sure to choose a network that will suit your temperament and interests. Some networks are large and noisy; others are quieter and many have specialized interests.

## 82 WHAT ARE CHANNELS?

Channels are where people talk to one another on IRC networks – you have to join a channel before you can take part. Every channel is run by an operator who has special powers, including setting the channel mode (most are public, but some have restricted access), and even controlling who is allowed on it.

**TALKING ON CHANNELS**

*In IRC networks, you can talk only to people on the same channel. You can switch channels to talk to different people, or have conversations going on several channels at once.*

*Channel operators have an @ symbol in front of their names. There may be more than one operator on a channel – particularly if it is very busy.*

*The channel name is always preceded by a # symbol.*

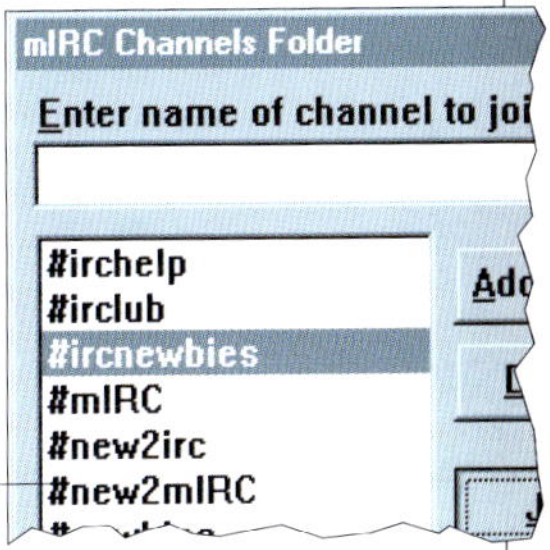


## 83 ACRONYMS & ABBREVIATIONS

Not everyone who joins in Internet Relay Chat can type very quickly, so a number of acronyms and abbreviations have been adopted as a form of shorthand to make life easier for participants.

**AFAIK**
As far as I know
**AFK**
Away from keyboard
**BCNU**
Be seeing you
**BRB**
Be right back
**BTW**
By the way
**CUL/CUL8R**
See you later

**FAQ**
Frequently asked question
**IMO**
In my opinion
**IMHO**
In my humble opinion
**LOL**
Laughing out loud
**MORF?**
Male or female?
**OAO**
Over and out

**OIC**
Oh I see
**RUOK**
Are you OK?
**SO**
Significant other
**THK**
Thanks
**TIA**
Thanks in advance
**WYSIWYG**
What you see is what you get

# 84 CONFIGURING AN IRC CLIENT PROGRAM

Whether you were supplied with an IRC client program by your provider or downloaded one from the Internet, you will have to configure it before connecting to a server for the first time. The steps below show you how to configure *mIRC*, a program you can download from **ftp://papa.indstate.edu/winsoc-l/Windows 95/IRC/**.

1 ◁ Connect to your service provider, then double-click *Mirc32* icon. *mIRC Setup* dialog box will now appear.

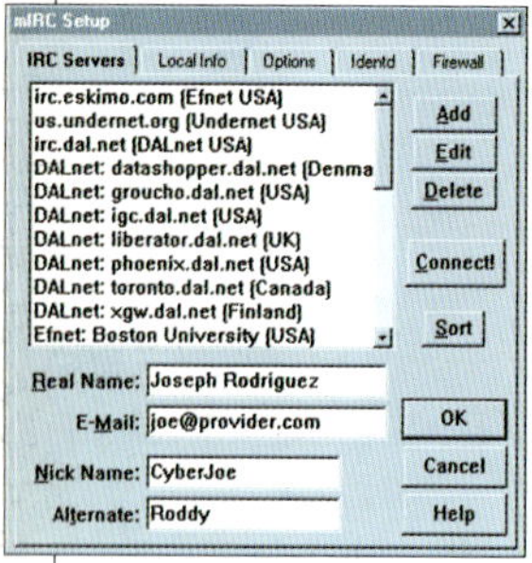


2 ◁ Click *IRC Servers* tab. Type your name, or an alias if you prefer, in *Real Name* box. Enter your e-mail address in *E-Mail* box. Type your nicknames in *Nick Name* and *Alternate* boxes. Finally click *Identd* tab.

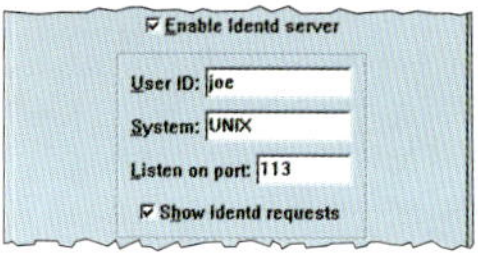


3 △ Check boxes next to *Enable Identd server* and *Show Identd requests.* In *User ID* panel, type your user name. Leave *System* as "Unix," and *Listen on port* as "113." Click *IRC Servers* tab.

4 ▷ Select name of server to which you want to connect (local server is likely to give faster connection). Finally, click *Connect* button.

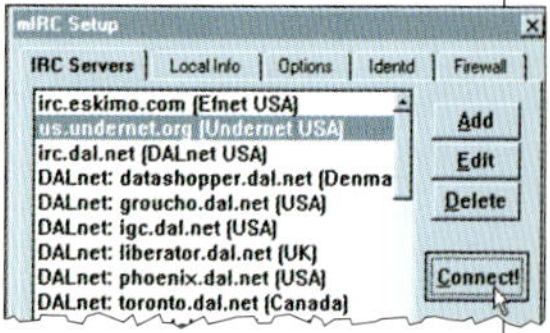


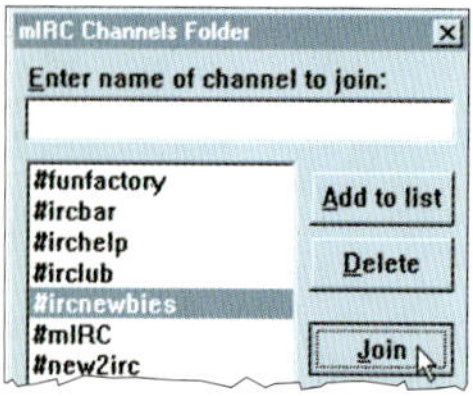


5 △ Click name of channel you want to join (here *#ircnewbies*), then click *Join* button.

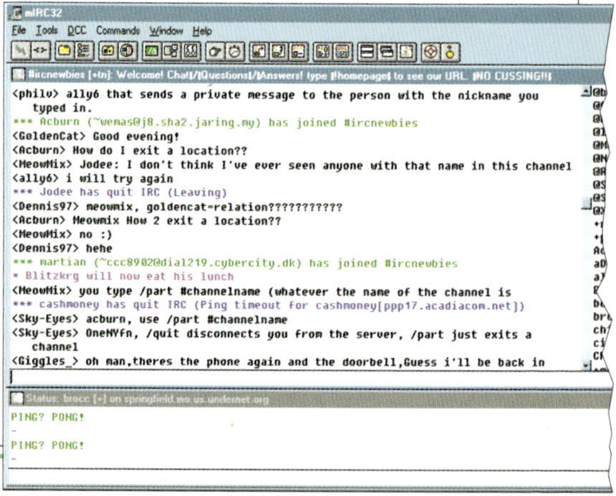


6 ▷ Messages for your channel will appear in new window. "Chat" by typing message in box at bottom of window and pressing Return key.

## 85 RUNNING AN IRC SESSION

Having configured your IRC client program (*mIRC* in this case) and joined a channel, the program's main window will appear ready for you to start a session. Some of the most important components of the *mIRC* interface are highlighted in the illustration below.

***Click on the setup button** to access the* mIRC Setup *dialog box.*

***To list all channels**, or for channel search, click this button. The* List Channels *dialog box will appear.*

***To set up direct** client-to-client connection, click here. This allows direct, exclusive talk with one other person.*

***Disconnect from IRC server***

***Connect to IRC server***

***All messages** for a channel appear in the channel window. More than one channel can be open at the same time, and each one will have its own window.*

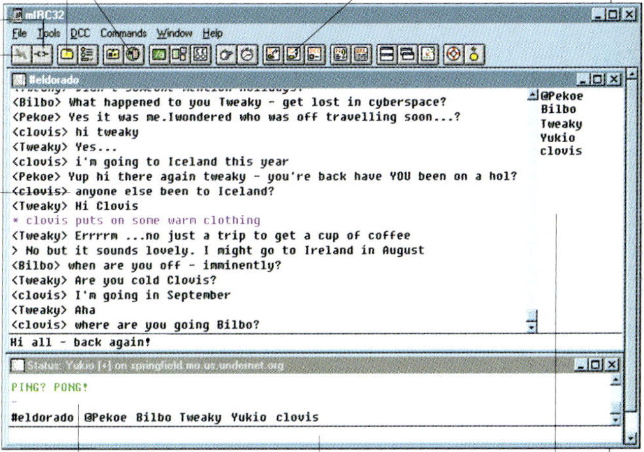


***The status window** tracks activity on the network, such as who has joined or left the network, and any server problems.*

***The single command line** at the bottom of each window is where you type your messages and IRC commands.*

***The right-hand panel** lists everybody who is currently connected to this particular channel.*

## 86 WATCH WHAT YOU TYPE!

If you are not sure what a command does, do not type it. It is possible for another user to take control of your program (and your hard disk) simply by asking you to type a password or command. The best policy is never to agree to type anything you don't understand.

# 87 CHATTING ON THE WEB

Although Web chat sites are rather slow compared to those run from an IRC program, chatting on the Web is usually more of a visual experience, and often allows you to include images and sounds with your message. There are hundreds of "live" chat sites on the Web, many offering a choice of places to talk.

△ IDENTIFY YOURSELF
*Most Web sites require you to identify yourself. Before joining the Globe site, for example, you must type a name and select a character icon for the session.*

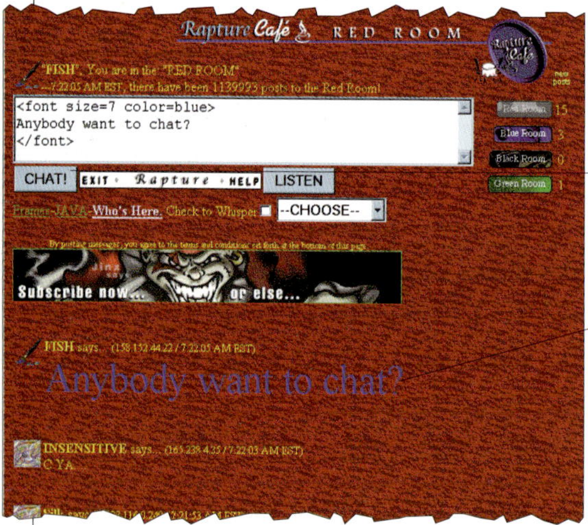


*At many sites you have to update the page manually to see new messages. For example, at the Globe site,* Listen *updates the message.*

*Most chat sites on the Web support HTML, which allows you to make your message more eyecatching by specifying details such as font size and color. The HTML code is shown above the* Chat *button.*

# 88 LOCATING WEB CHAT SITES

To locate Web chat sites, try the Web Broadcasting Service (at **http://www.wbs.net**), which has over 100 links to other Web chat sites. Alternatively you could try running a search for "chat" on one of the Web search engines or browse the categorized listings of sites that some of them provide.

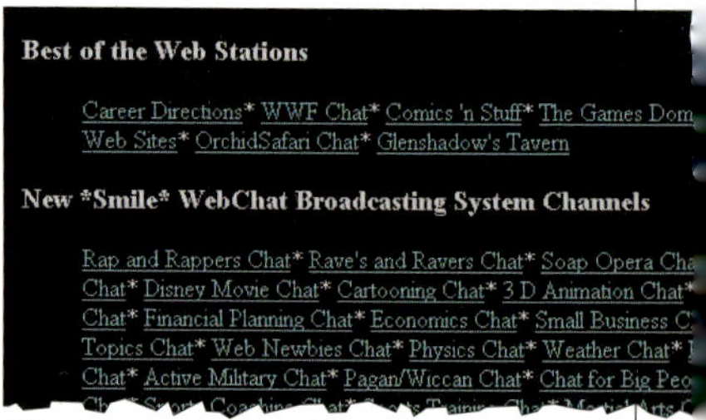


WEB BROADCASTING SERVICE
*WBS lists hundreds of good jumping-off points and has its own chat rooms.*

## 89 EXPLORING ON-LINE VIRTUAL WORLDS

An exciting new dimension has been added to the world of on-line chatting with the arrival of "virtual multiuser environments" or "cyberworlds." These virtual worlds, which combine elements of on-line chatting and graphic adventure games, are created with VRML (Virtual Reality Mark-up Language), which allows 3-D images to be displayed and manipulated on Web pages.

## 90 CHOOSE A WORLD

Several VRML sites on the Web provide information about virtual worlds. Try *Site of the Week* (**http://www.virtus.com/vrmlsite.html**) for up-to-date descriptions and reviews. *Superscape*'s home page provides a link to their *SuperCityII*, while other VRML worlds and models can be viewed using the *Viscape* browser plug-in.

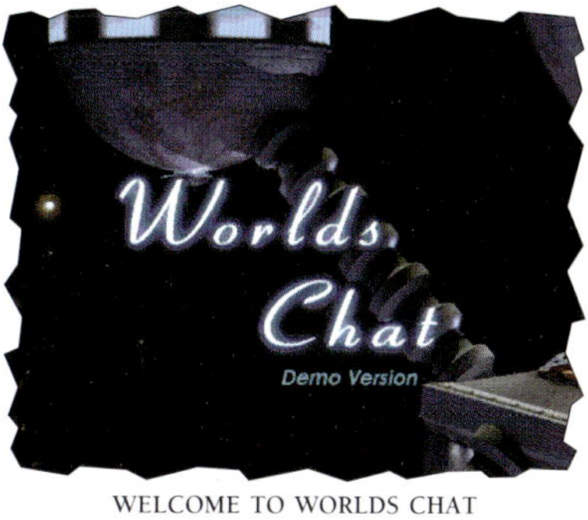


WELCOME TO WORLDS CHAT

## 91 DOWNLOADING WORLDS CHAT

Download the *Worlds Chat Demo* software from the Worlds Inc. site at **http://www.worlds.net**. At this site you will also find help files and other information relating to *Worlds Chat*. You will need a fast 486 PC with 8 MB of RAM to run *Worlds Chat* effectively.

## 92 CHOOSE A WORLDS CHAT AVATAR

In the on-line virtual world of *Worlds Chat*, individual users are represented by avatars, with whom other users can interact. Choose your avatar from a selection of portraits hanging in the Avatar Gallery, and log on to the *Worlds Chat* server, as explained below.

1 ▷ With arrow keys and mouse, move around Avatar Gallery until you find a suitable image for your avatar and click on it. "Walking man" icon will appear in the lower right of screen, and frame of portrait will be highlighted.

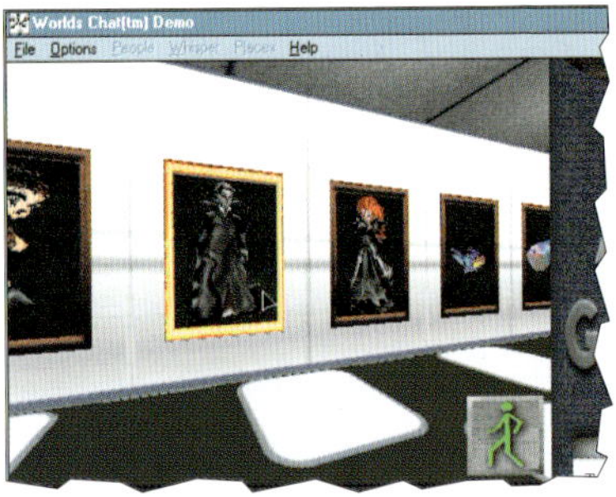


2 ▽ Click again on portrait for image to become rotating 3-D animation. Click *Accept* to choose this avatar.

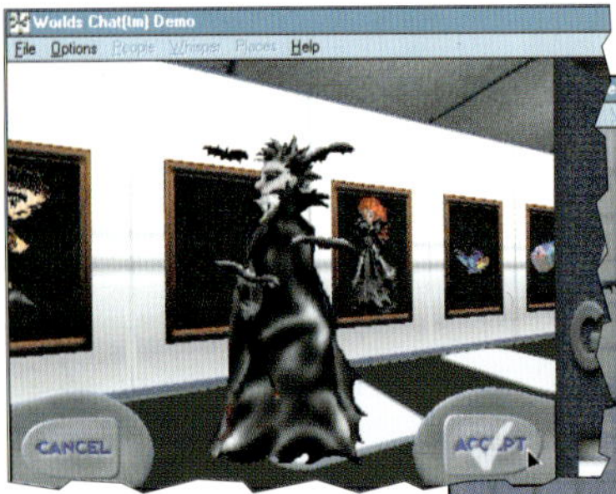


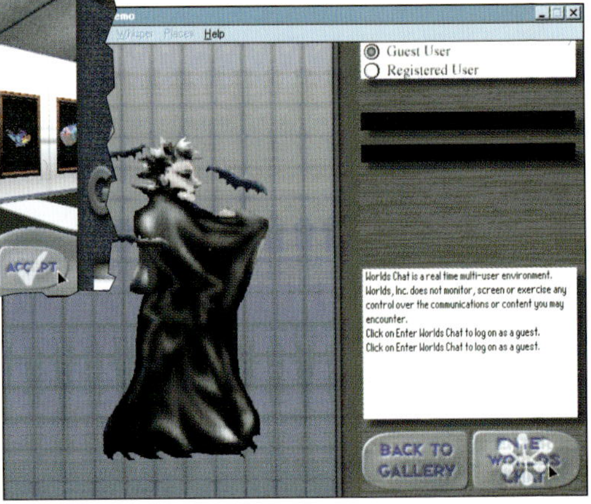


3 ▷ *Guest User* box will be checked. Click *Enter Worlds Chat* button to connect to *Worlds Chat* server and enter space station environment.

## 93 HOW TO COMMUNICATE

In *Worlds Chat*, you communicate with other users via the keyboard. Anything you "say" appears on screen for all users to read, unless you choose to communicate privately to a specific user by using the *Whisper to* option.

***The main screen** represents the space station from a first-person perspective. You can move around, interact with other avatars, and go through doors to explore.*

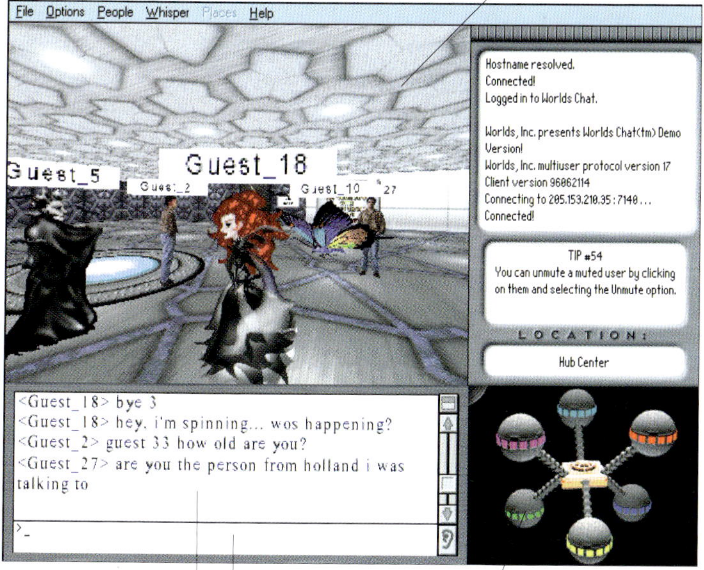


***The speech box** shows all speech as well as the names of the speakers. "Whispered" chat does not appear here, however.*

***To chat with other users,** type your words in the input box, then transmit them by pressing the Return key.*

***Click any of the globes** to teleport to a different location. Return to the Hub Center by clicking the center of the map.*

## 94 CAN YOU SPEAK PRIVATELY?

If you would like to speak privately to a *Worlds Chat* user, just click on that person's avatar and choose *Whisper to* from the drop-down menu. Alternatively, type the avatar's name, followed by a colon.

## 95 EXPLORING THE ENVIRONMENT

To explore the environment of *Worlds Chat*, you simply use the direction keys on your keyboard to move forward, backward, left, and right, using the mouse to make fine adjustments. Clicking on the screen suspends all movements, and a "walking man" icon appears. To resume movements once more, click on this icon.

**ROOMS & CORRIDORS**
Worlds Chat *is based on the idea of a space station. It contains rooms with different themes, which are linked by corridors, escalators, and elevators.*

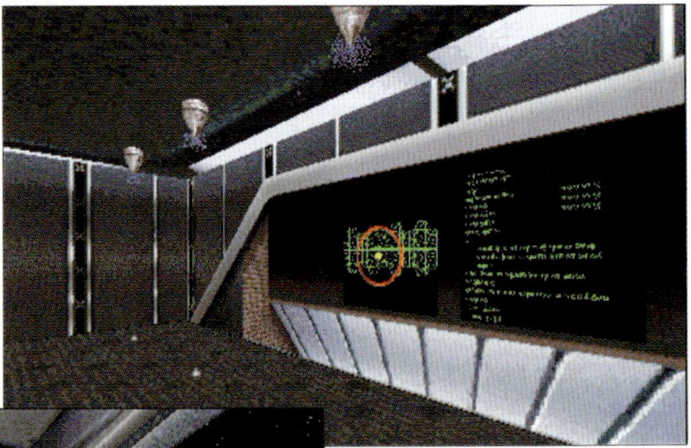

ENGINEERING CONTROL CENTER ▷

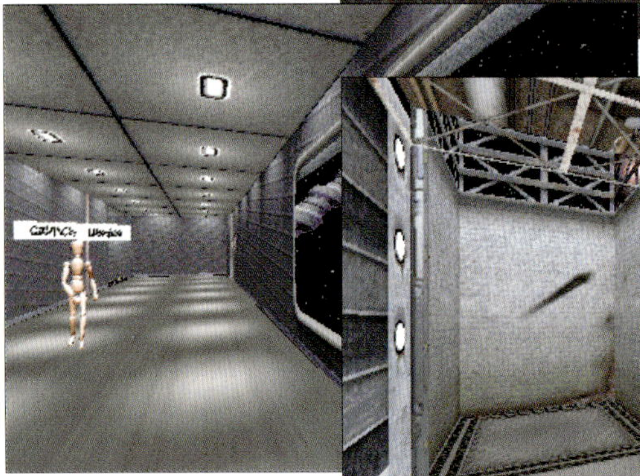

AIR WALK CORRIDOR ▽

WATER LIFT ▷

## 96 ENTERING WORLDSAWAY

*WorldsAway* is available only to *CompuServe* subscribers, and you will also need the *WorldsAway* software from *CompuServe*. To enter *WorldsAway*, connect to *CompuServe*, click the traffic light icon on the menu bar, type **away** in the *Go* box, then press Return.

## 97 WorldsAway avatars

As in other virtual worlds, *WorldsAway* users are represented by avatars, which are capable of a range of movements and gestures. Users can alter their avatars' clothing, color, and even their heads and bodies.

Your Avatar
*Your avatar can give any impression you want to convey to other users, by choice of clothing, gestures, and expressions.*

## 98 Communicating in WorldsAway

In the *WorldsAway* city of Phantasus, there are various areas devoted to different activities or themes. This is where people meet and communicate, as shown in the examples illustrated below.

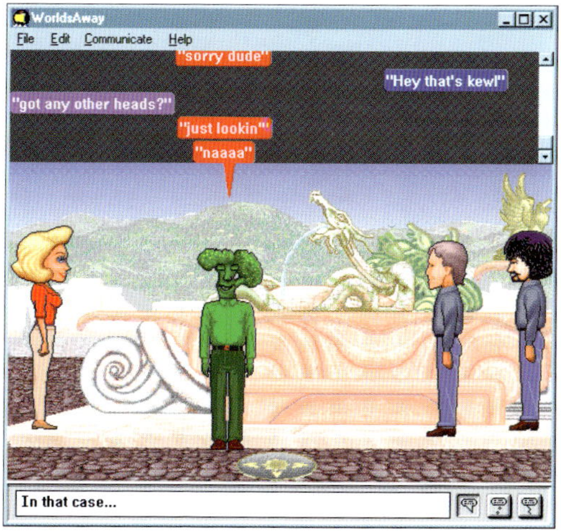


◁ Look Who's Talking
*Each avatar's words are displayed on the screen in a different color, so it is easy to identify a speaker. Click on an avatar to find out his or her name.*

△ Ghosting
*If you choose to become a ghost, you can "lurk" or eavesdrop without joining in the discussion yourself. A cloud icon represents your presence.*

△ Moving Around
*Movement is controlled by menus. Click on the ground, an avatar, or an object to access a menu with choice of movements.*

Keyboard Chat ▽
*In* WorldsAway, *you "talk" by typing in the speech box. You have three options: to talk aloud, to think, or to ESP. Thoughts appear in a "thinks" bubble; ESP is for private messages. You can ESP someone on a different screen if he or she is currently in the "dreamscape."*

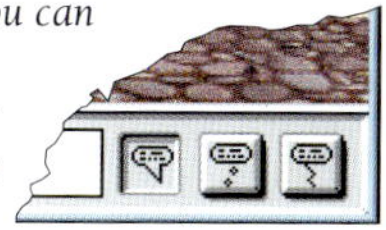

# 99 MONEY EXCHANGE IN WORLDSAWAY

A good deal of the activity in *WorldsAway* revolves around its token-based economy. On entering the world, you are given tokens, which you can spend in various ways. You "earn" more tokens by spending time in *WorldsAway* and by winning competitions.

◁ CHECK YOUR BALANCE
*Use an Automated Token Machine (ATM) to check your account or to withdraw tokens.*

◁ PAWN MACHINE
*If you are short of tokens, you can sell something at the pawn machine. You can even sell your avatar's head if you want to buy a new one.*

△ CHANGE HOW YOU LOOK
*To change your avatar's appearance, you can buy a new head or body, or body paint, at one of the vending machines.*

◁ GO SHOPPING
*Spend your tokens at one of the "vendroid" vending machines.*

# 100 ADDING A PHYSICAL DIMENSION

In *WorldsAway*, each avatar can display a range of gestures, actions, and facial expressions – all chosen from a drop-down menu or by pressing a function key – to convey emotion and humor.

HAPPY SAD ANGRY

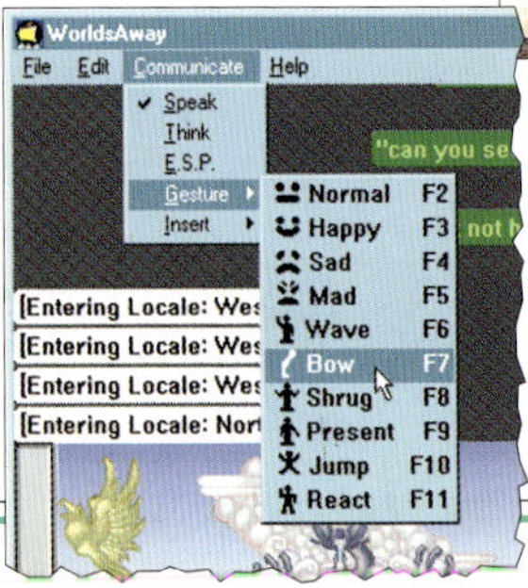

SHRUG WAVE BOW

◁ TAKE A BOW
*Let your avatar shrug, wave, or take a bow: simply click on the drop-down menu for an instant gesture.*

# 101 ON-LINE GAMING & PLUG-INS

With the plug-in games available for *WorldsAway*, you can play on-line against other avatars. Other activities are advertised in the *Kymer Clarion*, a *WorldsAway* newsletter. More details are available from the *Community Forum*.

▽ BINGO
*Host avatar will explain the rules, call the numbers, and award the prizes.*

JOINING A GAME ▷
*When new game starts, click* Register *button, and follow host's instructions.*

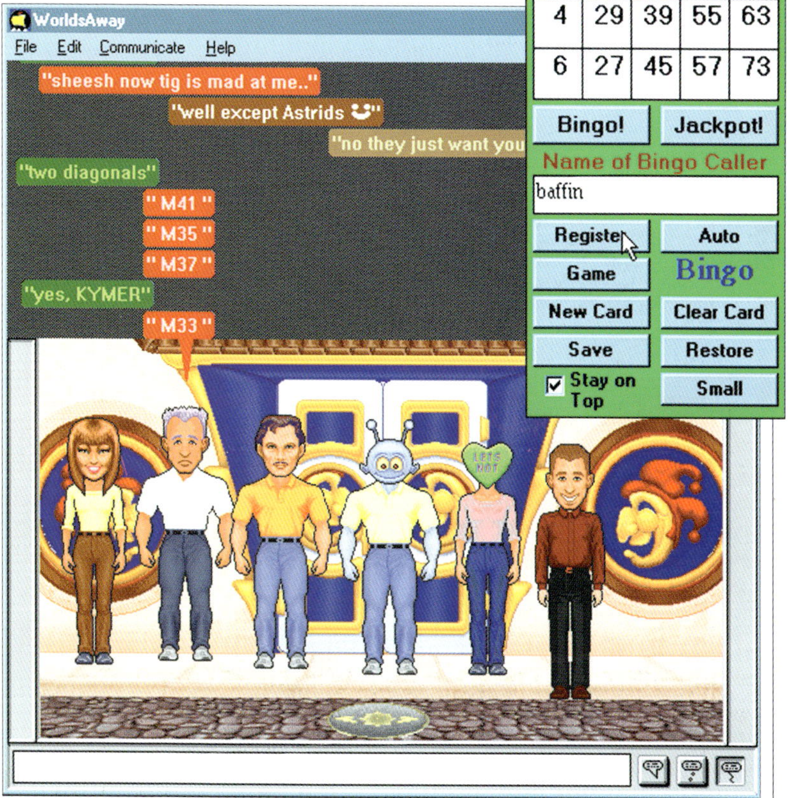

# INDEX

# ACKNOWLEDGMENTS

**Dorling Kindersley** would like to thank Hilary Bird for compiling the index, Fiona Wild for proof-reading and editorial help, Robert Campbell and Mark Bracey for DTP assistance, Sam Ruston for picture research, and Brian Cooper, Nigel Coath, Tim Mann, and Anna Milner for their invaluable help and advice.

**Photography**

KEY: t *top*; b *below*; c *center*; a *above*; l *left*; r *right*

The publisher would like to thank the following for their kind permission to reproduce their photographs: Cyberia Paris, one of Cyberia's global chain of Internet cafés, photo/Frederik Fourment 22cl; Robert Harding Picture Library/Warren Faidley 5tr; The Image Bank/Garry Gay 5tr; NASA/JPL 1, 5bc, 7tr, 31br, 48tr, 50–51; NCSA/UIUC 11tr; Copyright © 1996 PhotoDisc, Inc. 2; Telegraph Colour Library 36br, 54bl.

**Illustrations**

The publisher would like to thank the following copyright holders for their kind permission to reproduce their screengrabs/products, all of which are trademarks: © Lee Burton www.wintermute.net/pic.html 44b; permission granted by CompuServe Incorporated. Thank you to CompuServe (Information Services) UK for their help 66–67, 68–69; Condé Net/Condé Nast Publications, Inc. 40; Digital, AltaVista and the AltaVista logo are trademarks of Digital Equipment Corporation. Used with permission 47tr, cl, cr, br; Copyright © 1996 by Excite Inc. 38bc; Copyright © 1995, 1996 Forte Advanced Management Software, Inc. All Rights Reserved 5cb, 31cr, 55, 56; © Globalscape, Inc. 30b, 34–35, 36tr, c; Copyright © Hollywood Online Inc. 38ca; The Multimedia Newsstand is a service of the Hearst Corporation. All Rights Reserved, The Hearst Corporation 39tr; IUMA 44cla; Jeff Kuhn 47bl; mIRC Co. Ltd 59, 60–61; MSN is a trademark, and Microsoft, MS-DOS, and Windows are registered trademarks of Microsoft Corporation. Screenshots reprinted with permission from Microsoft Corporation 13tl, 16–17, 18–19, 42, 43tr, bl, 44r; Netscape Communications Corporation has not authorized, sponsored, or endorsed, or approved this publication and is not responsible for its content. Netscape and the Netscape Communications Corporate logos are trademarks and trade names of Netscape Communications Corporation. All other product names and/or logos are trademarks of their respective owners 10, 32l, 44bc, 45c, 47tr, cr, br, bl; Copyright © 1996 Netscape Communications Corp. All Rights Reserved. This page may not be reprinted or copied without the express written permission of Netscape 5bl, 8cb, 30tr, 31c, 38bl, 39cl, 43br, 48bl, br, 49, 52, 53bl; Brandon Plewe front cover cl, cb, 9cl; © Progressive Networks. All Rights Reserved 10tr, c, 44clb; Qualcomm Incorporated inside front flap b, 25, 26–27, 28–29; © RadioX/ Video On Line/ 10bl; © 1996 Superscape VR plc 45c; Teleport Internet Services 39cr; © UUNET PIPEX 1996 36tr; John Walker front cover cr, 9tr, 38cla; Web Broadcasting Service © 1996 WebChat Communications Inc. All Rights Reserved 62br; full title to all copyrights is owned by WebGenesis Inc. (607) 255-7724 (USA) 62–63; © 1996 WGN-TV front cover crb, 9cb, 38cra; David Woakes 32; Worlds Chat Screen Grabs © 1996, World's Inc. 63, 64–65; WSB-TV/Atlanta, Ga front cover ca, 9tl, 38cb; WRQ 38cl, crb.

Every effort has been made to trace the copyright holders. The publisher apologizes for any unintentional omissions and would be pleased, in such cases, to place an acknowledgment in future editions.